LESSONS
from a
FATHER
to His Son

LESSONS
from a
FATHER
to His Son

JOHN ASHCROFT

with Gary Thomas

THOMAS NELSON PUBLISHERS
Nashville

Published in Nashville, Tennessee, by Thomas Nelson, Inc., Publishers.

Unless otherwise noted, Scripture quotations are from THE NEW KING JAMES VERSION. Copyright © 1979, 1980, 1982, 1990, Thomas Nelson, Inc., Publishers.

Scripture quotations noted KJV are from the King James Version.

Excerpt from "The Creation" from GOD'S TROMBONES. Copyright © 1927 The Viking Press, Inc., renewed © 1955 by Grace Nail Johnson.Reprinted by permission of Viking Penguin, a division of Penguin Putnam, Inc.

Author's Note: The poem "It Couldn't Be Done," by Edgar A. Guest, which appears in Chapter 12, was taken from *The Collected Verse of Edgar A. Guest* (Chicago: Reilley and Lee Publishers, 1934), p. 285. The book has since gone out of print and the original publishing company is no longer in business. All attempts were made to contact the poet and/or his estate for permission to reprint, but were unsuccessful. The song "Keep Me True," which appears in Chapter 12, was composed by Mellie Mays. All attempts were made to contact the composer for permission to reprint, but were unsuccessful. The author wishes to thank the Assemblies of God music headquarters for its help in trying to secure permission for this song.

Library of Congress Cataloging-in-Publication Data
Ashcroft, John D., 1942–
    Lessons from a father to his son / John Ashcroft.
        p.   cm.
    ISBN 0-7852-7540-1
    1/ Ashcroft, John D., 1942–   —Family. 2. Legislators—United States—Biography. 3.
Ashcroft, John D., 1942–   —Philosophy. 4. Ashcroft, J. Robert—Philosophy. 5. Fathers—
United States—Biography. 6. United States. Congress. Senate—Biography. I. Title.
E840.8.A84A3   1998
328.73'092—dc21
[B]   98–10178
                                                                                                    CIP

Printed in the United States of America.

1 2 3 4 5 6 QPK 03 02 01 00 99 98

To my wife, Janet, and all the other moms and dads who realize that the transmission of values from one generation to the next is the single most important responsibility of a culture.

CONTENTS

Contents

Contents

ACKNOWLEDGMENTS

Virtually no aspect of this book could have been achieved by me alone. In the following paragraphs I attempt to highlight some of the many friends whose help was crucial, but a complete acknowledgment would rival the book itself.

Thanks be to God for giving me a childhood family that highlighted the inspiring values and life of my father. It goes without saying that I could not write about my father had God not graced me with such a parent. And God "graced" my father literally, with my mother, Grace. Her simple hard work and devotion to the practical released my father to focus on things eternal—and for that she is now enjoying her eternal reward.

My late brother Wesley lived in Springfield near my father and ministered to him so compassionately that together with my step-mother, Mabel, they elongated my father's life to my very substantial benefit. My father's last hours were spent with my brother Bob whose attention to my father gave him great pleasure. And Joy Collins, the unofficial daughter Mom and Dad loved so much, reminds me daily of the values and virtues that Dad pressed on all of us.

During my forties, I started meeting regularly with a group of my comtemporaries whose lives were also molded by my father. Dick Foth, Bob Cooley, George Wood, Wayne Kraiss, Don Argue, and others collectively known as the Bennett Springs Coalition, deserve my thanks for their assistance in helping me recollect incidents and events in which they shared.

My wife, Janet, read the manuscript carefully to elevate its accuracy, and she spent countless hours researching items in family memorabilia.

With great pleasure I acknowledge the very substantial assistance and help of Gary Thomas, whose capacity to grasp instantly my intentions and rightly integrate the various thoughts and lessons into a coherent whole was invaluable. His relaxed demeanor allowed us to endure a significant number of very long days and late nights in working and reworking my efforts to shape these lessons. It is no exaggeration to state that this book would not have happened without him.

The press of activity that has characterized my responsibilities has undoubtedly made "photographic" accuracy in this effort virtually impossible, but every effort has been made to get the facts right to the best of my abilities—though in some instances a few names and identifying details have been intentionally changed.

LIFE
LESSONS

———

*J*ohn, I'd like you to fly this plane for a while."

I was eight years old at the time, blue-jeaned and T-shirted and wide-eyed at the world. My father was an amateur pilot, and he had taken me to the sleepy Springfield airport, once a World War II training field. We walked up to a 1940s Piper Cub airplane. There wasn't much to it. It had a Tinkertoy-like frame, and it was covered not with metal, but with a painted-and-patched canvas.

Dad lifted me into the front seat. I watched him walk to the front of the plane, yell "Clear!" and throw the prop into motion. The plane shook and rumbled beneath me as Dad jumped in.

We went up in the air, and I was one awestruck kid. I was thousands of feet up in the air, and the stick frame and patched fabric under my shoes were the only things between me and a very hard ground!

And then my father shouted those unbelievable words over the engine's deafening roar: "John, I'd like you to fly this plane for a while."

I was going to fly the airplane! I looked around me at the spartan interior, which was nothing at all like the multitudinous controls, gauges, and computerized equipment in planes today. The control stick looked like a broom handle and came up between my legs. That little stick was all I needed to move us up, down, left, or right.

"What do I do?" I shouted back to my father, who was seated behind me.

"Just grab the stick and push it straight forward."

"Okay." I took hold of that stick and did as I was told. Immediately the plane went into a straight bombing-raid dive toward a farm on the outskirts of Springfield! My stomach came up to my throat and I lost all sense of time or place as fear gripped my insides. I let go of that control stick in a millisecond, and Dad pulled the plane back up.

He had a good chuckle, and I had a good lesson: actions have consequences. I learned in a particularly vivid—in fact, terrifying—way that my decisions and actions could imperil my future. In a positive sense, I learned that wherever I was, if

I put my hand to something, I could make a difference. The context and emotion surrounding this lesson were such that I would never forget it.

My childhood was filled with such lessons, given by a man who grew into spiritual greatness. Many of you, perhaps most, have never heard of him, but hardly a week goes by that somebody does not come up to me and recount a poignant tale concerning my father.

In many ways Dad was a very ordinary man. He never ran for political office, never built a business, never made a mark on Wall Street. He served as a pastor and then as president of several colleges—a respectable vocational path, certainly, but not one the media might identify as historic. Yet I believe that a sincere, unaffected life can be a profound life, and a quiet, courageous, and faithful obedience can be far more inspiring than a clamorous pursuit of fame. My father's life demonstrated this truth.

This is a book that celebrates the fundamental, the quiet, and the routine. It's the story of a father's faith, a mother's mercy, and a son's aspiration. At the center of it is my father, J. Robert Ashcroft.

In the following pages I would like to introduce you to this man—not by telling you his life story, but by revealing vignettes that demonstrate his uncommon sense and unworldly wisdom. These principles challenged my life and shaped the lives of the many people he touched. As you join me on this journey, I trust that these insights will enrich your life as much as they have enriched mine.

You may have never heard of J. Robert Ashcroft, but once you finish this book, I believe you will never forget him.

NOBLE ASPIRATIONS

*J*n the year Richard Nixon was elected to a second term in office, the only announced candidate in my congressional district was a fellow by the name of Gene Taylor. At first glance, Gene was an easy guy to undervalue; but, in hindsight, that was part of his draw. He was a genuine Missourian, a Ford dealer from Sarcoxie, a small town in the southwest part of the district. Gene had a folksy demeanor and spent much of his time on the campaign trail telling stories and anecdotes—always making you laugh, sometimes making you blush.

I knew little about Gene, except that he had twice been elected the national committeeman from Missouri. He was deeply embedded in Republican Party politics, but I was as naive as they come in those days and didn't see this as the formidable obstacle that it was.

At the time I was teaching business law and law-related subjects, and I was somewhat bothered by the fact that nobody else was running except Gene. Political operatives did not share my frustration. In fact, I received a phone call inviting me to a rally on Gene's behalf.

"We want so many people to come out to the rally," the caller said, "that no one else will dare to run against Gene."

That got on my nerves. Democracy is supposed to be based on having good choices, and they wanted me to participate in a rally with the intended purpose of eliminating other choices.

The more I thought about this, the less I liked it, so I tried to get other people to run. My preferred choice was a local prosecutor. He was an immensely popular guy and I thought he would make a good legislator. He said he would give it careful consideration, so I thought my recruiting was over—until I received a call from him just one day before the filing deadline.

"Sorry, John," the prosecutor said. "I've decided not to run against Gene."

"Then who will?"

There was a long pause. "No one that I know of."

I sighed. It was a heavy sigh, the kind that often precedes precipitous action.

That night I asked that our family get together. We went to

my father's house and met in a room that had great meaning to me because of my childhood.

FATHER'S PRAYERS

So many years ago, as I eased out of the nether world of a seven year old's sleep, I heard those earnest but discordant tones that signaled my father's morning ritual. His words, punctuated with passion, made their way up to the second floor, greeting me as I fought my way back into the world of consciousness.

Dad's prayers were not the quiet, whispered entreaties of a timid Sunday school teacher. My father prayed as if his family's life and vitality were even then being debated on high as he bowed low.

Hearing him pray was a magisterial wake-up call. While many kids wake up to the smell of coffee brewing or the sound of a rooster crowing, I have cherished memories of entering the day as this man's outspoken prayers filtered throughout the house.

Sometimes I would ease downstairs and join him. One knee was usually raised, so I would slip in underneath him. In this way I was shielded by his body as he pleaded for my soul. Sitting so close to him provided a serenity and comfort that captivated my heart.

If there was extra time, he would play and sing hymns of the church on the piano. Mom made sure we never left for school without a fully satisfied stomach, but Dad was concerned with feeding our spirits, leaving a gospel tune embedded in our thoughts as we left the harbor so fondly known as home.

During these early morning times I never caught my father praying for our happiness—not that he was opposed to it. I never heard him pray for a bigger house or a bigger car or a bigger bank account. Instead, he prayed that our hearts would be ignited and inspired to do *noble* things, which would have eternal consequences. "Turn our eyes from the temporal, the physical, and the menial," he prayed, "and turn us toward the eternal, the spiritual, and the noble."

My dad had the foresight and wisdom not to say, "I just want my kids to be happy." He realized that the pursuit of happiness for its own sake is a frustrating, disillusioning, and often futile effort. Happiness usually hides from those who are spiritually addicted to its sugar, while it chases after those who make wise choices and who are caught up in something more lasting than momentary excitement.

My father never pressured us toward achievement. He knew that noble aspirations required noble motives, that, in fact, the push had to come from inner reserves, not outward designs. He simply dangled before us the possibilities of such accomplishments. Thanks to his example, we sometimes took the bait.

Dad understood a few things about motivation. I remember a statement he made while I was in college. "I don't care so much about whether you make As, Bs, or Cs," he said, much to my surprise, "but whether you *care* about making As, Bs, or Cs."

He was far more interested in my spirit than my performance, which I believe demonstrates a profound understanding of human nature. If a person adopts the right spirit, the performance levels will take care of themselves.

Maybe that's why, in 1972, I was so willing—quite honestly, foolishly so—to aspire to fill a seat in Congress.

In the very same room where my father knelt for morning prayers, our family now sat and discussed my possible candidacy. At seven o'clock, the family members decided to split up to pray for about half an hour, each of us choosing a separate part of the house. Thirty minutes later we came back together and talked it over some more. And then we made the choice: I ought to give it a try.

Today I smile when I think about my political poverty. At the time I couldn't even name all the counties in our district. I had never been to a Republican organizational meeting, and it was sheer folly to think I could take on one of the powers of the party and win.

But fools rush in where angels fear to tread, and I was going to try!

THE "WEALTHY" CANDIDATE

The campaign kicked into action the next morning, the last day on which I could file for candidacy. My younger brother, Wesley, offered to take my wife, Janet, and me down to Joplin so I could announce my candidacy there first. After that I would hold another press conference in Springfield, followed by yet a third in Jefferson City, where I would file for office in the state capitol.

We had to get up well before the chickens, as we planned to make our first announcement in Joplin—over an hour's drive away—at 5:30 in the morning. That was our first ridiculous mistake. Nobody ever attends a 5:30 A.M. press conference, especially one called by an unknown candidate whose press release does not go out until late the night before.

Miraculously, one reporter from a radio station showed up. I gave my spiel, then got onto a sparsely populated commercial flight around six o'clock, flying into Springfield minutes later. While I was in the air, Wes was making a mad dash past Springfield to Jefferson City—about two hundred miles away—so I would have someone to pick me up at the airport.

The press got the wrong idea when Janet and I were the only ones who got off the plane in Springfield. One of the reporters assumed that I had chartered the jet on my own, even though Janet and I had purchased regular tickets. News reports began to spread about the "independently wealthy" candidate who chartered a jet to announce his candidacy on a moment's notice.

Ironically, one of the reasons Wes was not still with me was that we could not afford round-trip tickets, and I needed a car and driver in Jefferson City to get me home. It was a funny feeling to be considered a wealthy candidate; I just wished it were my banker making the statement!

A few more reporters showed up at Springfield as Wes sped to the capital. Our organization might have looked formidable, but it consisted entirely of two brothers trying to do their best with a used car and a one-way plane ticket. The highways weren't in anywhere near the condition they are now, so Wes had a tough job. If he did not meet my flight into central Missouri, our "organization" could fall on its face—in front of the state's most important political reporters.

At the capitol in Jefferson City, I said that I wanted to make an "American election" out of this race. "The definition of an American election is that you get a choice," I said. "The Communists have elections, but they have only one candidate on the ballot. It shouldn't be that way in America, so I'm announcing my candidacy for the Republican nomination to represent this district in Congress."

My "platform" would surely need to develop, but I believed

in what I was doing, and my father had programmed me to aspire to noble things, even if they were not fully realistic.

Though I lost that primary race, it led to something I never could have imagined, which taught me the depth of wisdom in my father's insistence that we aspire to noble things. A failed attempt is not necessarily a dead end; it can be a way station on the path to something even better.

Three

FOR EVERY CRUCIFIXION

$\mathcal{M}$y theory about elections is mirrored in what I hold about all of life: for every crucifixion, a resurrection is waiting to follow—perhaps not immediately, but the possibility is there. I have always been impressed by the ministry of Fulton Buntain, a Tacoma, Washington, pastor, who passed out bumper stickers to his congregation. The stickers read, "IT'S NEVER TOO LATE TO START OVER AGAIN," and "IT'S ALWAYS TOO SOON TO QUIT."

I had garnered about 45 percent of the vote in the 1972 primary campaign for Congress, and as I reviewed the returns, a clear pattern emerged: our support was strong but too narrow. I had gotten better than a two-to-one majority in my home, the Springfield metropolitan area, but was totally whacked most everywhere else, losing close to four to one at the other end of the district.

I went back to teaching college students, preparing to settle into the quiet but comfortable life of a college professor and gentleman farmer. But God had other plans.

One evening I was sitting at a little dining room table in our rock house. The house itself was smaller than a double-wide trailer, but it was beautifully situated on a piece of land bisected by the Little Sac River. The phone rang, and when I answered it, Dr. Gaynard Graham, my dentist and the president of our local Rotary club, was on the other end.

"John David," he began, and I smiled. Boyhood friends know things about you that nobody else does, including the way your mother used to address you.

Gaynard continued, "We just saw this guy Kit Bond get elected governor, and we need to get him down here to talk to our Rotary club. I was thinking you might know him, since you were in the primary. Think you could give him a call and invite him?"

I thought the chances of Kit Bond knowing me were no better than fifty-fifty.

"I don't know, Gaynard," I confessed. "I lost the primary, after all, and I don't think I ever did much more than give a banquet invocation when he was present, but let me see what Janet thinks."

I cupped my hand over the phone and called out, "Janet? If I ran into Kit Bond on the street, would he know me?"

"I think so," Janet said. "After all, you campaigned together at some of the same fairs; I think he'd know you."

I took my hand off the phone and spoke back to Gaynard. "Well, Janet thinks Kit would know me, so I'll see if I can get a call through and invite him."

I had only started back to the dining room table when the phone rang again.

"John?" the voice asked. "This is Kit Bond."

I cupped my hand over the phone and called out to Janet, "Hey, he knows me!"

"Who?" she asked.

"Kit Bond! He's on the phone!"

Janet started laughing as I turned my attention to the surprise caller. Kit asked me, "Have you ever thought of going into state government? We're going to need a lot of good people in this administration."

"Well, Kit," I said, "I didn't run for state office, I ran for Congress—and I lost."

"Well, you ought to think about state government. We'll need a lot of good help here in the capital, John. So if you don't mind, would you please send up a résumé?"

"Sure, I'll send you one. I'd be honored to. By the way, if you can see your way clear to speak at our Rotary club, we'd sure appreciate it."

"I'll see what I can do."

That was the last time I thought about it, until about a week later when a university secretary buzzed me at my desk. "John," she said, "Governor-elect Kit Bond is on the phone."

I remembered my promise about the résumé and flinched. "Ask if he would hold for just a minute," I said.

When he acquiesced, I told my secretary, "Quick, get a copy of my résumé and put it in an envelope, addressing it to Kit. I need to tell him it's coming his way."

She got the résumé, then put me through to Kit.

After the pleasantries Kit finally asked, "John, how old are you?"

"I'm thirty."

"Are you sure?"

"Well, you know, Governor, I'm not sure about a lot of things in life, but this one I'm pretty clear on."

Through my door I could see the secretary drop the envelope containing my résumé in the mail. "By the way," I added, "I want you to know that I haven't forgotten about that résumé. It's on its way."

"Okay," he said, and hung up. Once again, I put the conversation out of my mind. It did not dawn on me that you had to be thirty years old to be the state auditor of Missouri. Nor did I put that together with the fact that Kit had been the state auditor when he ran for governor. Since the auditor is elected during a different election in the off years, Kit would soon need to appoint someone to his old office.

Another week or so went by when I got a third call from Kit. "John," he said, "how would you like to be the state auditor of Missouri?"

"I don't know what a state auditor does," I answered. "I'm an attorney, not an accountant."

"That's all right," Kit said. "I can teach you what you need to know; I wasn't an accountant when I got started either."

"Hmmm," I said.

How is that for an enthusiastic response!

"Well, think it over," Kit said. "I'm going to Scottsdale, Arizona, for the weekend. A new governors' conference is going on out there. Let's get back together on this."

Kit must have been mystified by my lackadaisical response. I did not understand that the state auditor was the fourth-ranking executive official in the state of Missouri! The newspapers were full of all kinds of speculation about whom the new governor might appoint for which positions—you've seen those articles, the kinds with rows of pictures and short biographies. The greatest speculation was over who would be appointed state auditor, but I was not being mentioned.

I called a few close friends—it was to be a highly

confidential situation—and asked them what they thought, and only then did I realize some people would practically kill for such an appointment. Years later, during my two administrations as governor, I was stunned by the way people fought desperately for even low-level appointments. They would organize letter-writing campaigns, generating sometimes two or three hundred letters in support of their appointment.

Here I was being handed the fourth-ranking job in the state without even asking for it! From one perspective, it just fell into my hands.

But there's another side. When you pursue noble things, sometimes noble things pursue you. If I had not run for Congress and lost, there would not have been an appointment. Once I saw what Kit was offering me, I could not have been more grateful. No way was this chap going to pass up the chance to be the fourth-ranking executive officeholder in Missouri, particularly when the guy who held it before me had just been elected governor!

If losing the election for Congress was a crucifixion, then my appointment as state auditor was a resurrection. The state auditor is a *statewide* responsibility; there are nine congressional representatives in Missouri, but only one state auditor.

While my father did not teach me to respect Hollywood and its stars, I like Errol Flynn's maxim that he'd rather be sorry at the close of his life for the things he had done than the things he hadn't done. Though Errol may have put his own saucy twist on that, there is some truth embedded in his statement. It reminds me of Teddy Roosevelt and his aspiration to be part of "the fellowship of doers."

The doers of this life might fail; my father had his vocational setbacks just like everyone else. But doers never let the fear of failure or even actual failure keep them down.

Think of the way our national pastime, major-league baseball, has reinvigorated itself. After a long marriage, our country's relationship with baseball began to sour. The sport hit the bottom in the early '90s during a players' strike, and many wondered if baseball was dead. Along came Cal Ripken Jr., the new Iron Man. And Ken Griffey Jr. and Mark McGwire, as they launched a tremendous assault on Roger Maris's single-season home run record in 1997. Soon our nation was once again patronizing the boys of summer.

There is not a single business, individual, or church that has not had seasons of failure. Just because we are called to aspire does not mean we are called always to succeed. Even the best players do not get hits every time they step up to the plate, but my father was a man who inspired us to respond to "Batter up" regardless of circumstances—and I'm glad he did.

As the years rolled by, there would be more elections, some not so successful, and other elections successful beyond my wildest imagination. But at the relatively young age of thirty, I woke up and realized my father had programmed me to be a part of that fellowship of doers, and that is a gift I still treasure today. There are few things more profound that a father can give his children than the aspiration to noble meaning.

My congressional election loss did not end at a crucifixion; it became a resurrection, and an open door to my lifelong vocation of public service.

But other crucifixions lay ahead.

CHAPTER
Four

DO
OR DIE

———

*R*epublicans were not having a good year in 1974. Both the president and vice president had resigned during my campaign to be elected state auditor, the office to which Kit had appointed me just two years before. Now I was running for a second term as auditor. One incident in particular gave me a vivid picture of what I was up against.

"What party did you say you were from?" the man asked me.

"I'm a Republican," I said confidently.

Without saying another word, the man gathered his saliva and spat on me. I took out a handkerchief and said to myself, "This could be a long campaign."

It was, and, ultimately, an unsuccessful one. Though I had held the fourth-highest state office at the young age of thirty, I had yet to win an election by the age of thirty-three.

Another two years went by. It was 1976, and I decided to run for the office of state attorney general. It looked to me like a do-or-die election. And it was a tough, tough battle. That year our incumbent Republican governor, Kit Bond, narrowly lost his bid for reelection. Jimmy Carter handily defeated our incumbent Republican president, Gerald Ford. I was running against a very qualified individual who, frankly, would have been an excellent attorney general. As a Democrat, he had serious differences with me, but I respected him and could understand why people supported him.

Looking back, I'm not sure why I kept running, except that my father had instilled in me a particular set of values, which I believed needed to be reinforced by government leaders. I was so committed to these values, I was willing to endure the risk of sure political death if I encountered an embarrassing third consecutive loss.

It's not that I believed I needed to hold office to practice leadership. My parents certainly did not believe this. Years later, after I had been elected to several offices, people would come up to my mother and inquire, "How's your son doing?"

Mom was always quick to reply, "I have *three* sons." She and Dad were wise enough to know that there is no hierarchy of value based on how often you get your name in the papers. True leadership is much more universal than that.

LEADERSHIP

Fresh out of law school as a college teacher, I recognized the opportunity to practice what I call "intensive leadership." As long as there is somebody whom you are influencing, you are a leader. Even a ten-year-old girl is a leader if she has a younger brother or sister who looks up to her. In fact, I believe that virtually every person is the most important leader to at least one other person in the world.

As my children were growing up, Janet and I were certainly the most important leaders in their world—more important leaders than the president of the United States, the secretary general of the United Nations, or the leader of the Soviet bloc. Each of us is required to exercise leadership, even if that is "intensive" leadership, limited to our personal relationships.

But there is another kind of leadership my father taught me: an "extensive" leadership, which reaches beyond a few close relationships to influence the community and culture. I saw my father display this kind of leadership around the world.

As a college teacher, I had an opportunity to help reinforce values and promote positive character traits to about two hundred students every semester. But once you have had a taste of even more extensive leadership, it's hard to let go. My short two-year stint as state auditor had given me that taste. I realized that there is a lot you can do to influence our culture as a governmental leader. For starters, your position gives you access to a public podium. For good or for ill, politicians can share ideas and concepts in a way not afforded to most in the private sector.

With this in mind, I decided to give the political scene one more try. I could not count my first election loss in 1972 as a total failure. Even though I lost that race, my candidacy had catapulted me to a level I had no earthly right to reach at that stage in life. And I realized there were other mitigating factors in the 1974 collapse that made running as a Republican particularly difficult; it was premature to write off such an opportunity of extensive leadership based on these two elections alone.

"One more try," I told my dad, and he smiled. "I'm going to give it one more try."

And that aspiration led to another resurrection.

ELECTED

I will never forget the night of my first victory. It was a tense, tough, and oftentimes traumatic evening. As I have already mentioned, 1976 was a year Republicans wished never happened; they were forced to pay a costly electoral price for Watergate.

My own race was in the balance all evening long. Janet and I had come to the hotel for the "victory party," which soon began to resemble a wake. Kit Bond had lost, President Gerald Ford was in the process of losing, and I was exhausted by the discouraging numbers in my own race.

At 1 A.M., I was behind by about 13,000 votes, with most of the votes already counted. Paper ballots were still common in those days, and it took a lot longer to count them. As I faced the very distinct possibility of losing my third election in a row, I hung on to the fact that I had given the campaign everything I could. With my work over, and nothing I could do to improve the outcome, I decided to go home and go to bed. I may have lost the election, I thought, but there's no sense in losing a good night's sleep.

About 5:30 that November morning, I woke up. It was a calm and quiet morning, a dark, cool predawn. My mind replayed the events of the previous evening as I rubbed my forehead, hoping to massage away the bad memories. It was unusual for me to wake up that early, but there I was, lying in bed, listening for a moment to the quiet.

"RRRIIINNNGGG!"

Was that the phone? I wondered. My dazzled brain danced into consciousness.

"RRRIIINNNGGG!"

That is *the phone!* It was the most welcome, glorious sound I had ever heard, because one thing is certain: nobody calls you at 5:30 A.M. to tell you you've lost!

I snatched up the receiver.

"Good news," Paul DeGregorio, my campaign guru, gushed. "The rural ballots have started to turn in our favor. We think you better come down here, because it looks like we've got a winner on our hands."

Hah! Yes!!!

Janet and I sprang out of bed, cleaned up, and went back to the hotel. I felt like a man who had been sentenced to political death the night before but who had been handed a reprieve in the early morning hours. Running as a Republican, I had won in a year in which Republicans were benched in droves.

While it's always more fun winning than losing, every time I have ever run for something and lost, some type of "resurrection" has followed. When I lost my race for Congress, I was appointed state auditor. After I lost my race to stay in as state auditor, I ended up running for, and winning, the position of attorney general. In the '90s, my failure to be elected chairman of the Republican National Committee led to my successful race for the United States Senate.

You could say there was actually an ascendance after every loss. We don't like the losses in life. They don't leave behind the sweet aftertaste of victory. Sometimes they leave us feeling nothing more than the sore muscles of defeat. But those sore muscles signify that growth is taking place, leading to something even better.

Here is what I learned from my dad: through the ups and

downs of failure and success, we become better people, and as better people, God can call us to bigger jobs. As we travel through the peaks of acclaim and the valleys of rejection, and as we watch our children do the same, we can take heart that it is the journey, not just the destination, that carries meaning and fulfillment.

Five

YOU DON'T SAY

$\mathcal{A}$s part of a long ministerial career, my father served as the president of a small, liberal arts college in the Midwest. After more than fifteen years, it appeared that his vision for the college's future differed somewhat from that of the board of trustees. I was never aware of any actual points of contention, but once my father realized that these differences were unlikely to be resolved, he told the trustees, "I don't want you to be unhappy with the person you have running the college, so I'll tender a letter of resignation."

This occurred in early fall. The board sat on this letter until late spring. Then, just days before commencement exercises in May, the board formally accepted his resignation.

If the board had waited a few dozen hours, a handful of days, my father could have handed out the diplomas and congratulated the graduating seniors he had known and loved as president of the college. As it was, the abrupt timing of his termination could easily have been construed as malicious.

Many students and not a few faculty were extremely upset. The students expected to get their diplomas from my father. After all, he had been their president for three years, eight months, and all but a few days of their academic careers!

Yet when my father called to tell me the news, he was remarkably dispassionate. It was all very matter-of-fact. "John, I thought you should know that I'm leaving the college. I submitted my resignation last autumn, and the board has chosen to act on it."

Remarkably, my father would not allow a single negative to enter our conversation. Though I tried to probe him and find out what had really happened, it was clear to me that he held no grudges. In fact, the posture he took astonished me. Instead of feeling bitter, my father had a profound sense of gratitude for the work he had enjoyed while serving as president of a college.

The controversy was aggravated because the board of trustees named a replacement within days. Normally it takes a good year or more to hire a new college president. This led some to wonder if my father had simply been held on until the board found a new president, and then, once the choice was made, he was let go instantly.

Dad was not blind to all this; he had been a college president for almost two decades, and though many suggested he had every reason to be upset, my father never reflected any of that. Neither did he ever complain. On the contrary, he continued to befriend and serve all of the individuals involved in the awkward decision to replace him days before the school term ended.

What my father *didn't* say about this situation told me as much about him as what he did say on many other occasions. I learned that he was a man who didn't nurse, feed, or build grudges.

I have seen people act very differently. Perhaps an employer fired or laid them off—and in many of these situations, the authorities making the request had every proper reason to do so. Even though the dismissals were handled fairly and with compassion, the dismissed parties chose to become bitter; they set up a competing operation or spent several months spreading poisonous bile about their former organization.

My father could have done that. It would be hyperbole to suggest that he was a "political power" in our denomination, but he was fairly well known, with good standing, and more than a few people looked up to him. They watched to see how he would react. If he had decided to seek vengeance or spread negative gossip, he would have found many willing ears. Instead, my father went out of his way to endorse every aspect of the college and even the individuals involved in terminating his service.

It may be that the board of trustees had legitimate reasons for asking my father to leave. Though it is hard to understand their timing, perhaps it was time for him to move on. But since there was no moral scandal to justify his abrupt and untimely dismissal, I think it's safe to say that many in my father's situation would have struggled mightily against feelings of being ill-used.

But again, my father told me a lot by what he didn't say. He didn't ask his family to bear the emotional strain and stress of his responsibilities while he served as president, and he wasn't about to change course, asking us to bear the strain of an indecorous dismissal. I've heard of fathers who come home in a rage when their employer has treated them unfairly; they have been made to suffer by their employer, and now their families must pay the price, their wives and children wilting under the heat of their pain.

That did not happen in my father's house. He seemed incapable of holding a grudge. This is a lesson that has served me well in public office.

TURNING OPPONENTS INTO FRIENDS

Early in my political career, I approached a popular state senator of my own party with whom I had worked closely as state auditor. I asked him to support me in my bid to be elected attorney general for the state of Missouri. He refused to commit his support, making it clear that I was too conservative for his taste.

"Sorry, John," he said. "I simply can't be a part of your campaign."

His endorsement would have made my election go much more smoothly, but I respected his choice and his honesty and went on to campaign as hard as I knew how.

As it turned out, I was elected, while he left the state senate and moved out-of-state to pursue a business opportunity. Later, when he returned to Missouri, he needed a job, and at that time I needed the kind of help he could bring to my office. I didn't even have to review his résumé. I knew he would be competent in the position and that Missouri would be well served by his appointment.

"You're hired," I told him.

He looked a little stunned. "It's a bit puzzling to me that after I wouldn't be part of your campaign, you're willing to make me a part of your office," he confessed. The truth of the matter is, I understood his refusal to support me and appreciated the honesty he had demonstrated in telling me so.

There have been other times when my father's legacy of not holding a grudge was more difficult to follow, even though his example ultimately prevailed. During my first campaign for the Republican nomination for governor, I faced the most formidable opponent I had ever run against. Without a doubt, this campaign was the toughest one of my life, eyeball-to-eyeball all the way.

Both my opponent and his campaign manager, Tracy Mehan, hit me with every legal shot and nearly every other shot that couldn't be proved illegal. There was no letup. For instance, my predecessor in the attorney general's office—a person of significant wealth—frequently requested no reimbursement for his expenses. The Mehan-directed campaign collected data comparing my level of official expenses as attorney general—which I turned in—with my predecessor's expenses as attorney general, in order to cast me as a "reckless, wasteful" public servant. The truth was that my predecessor had quite similar expenses but just didn't submit them. That point, however, was never made.

It was a tough campaign; there was no time to sleep when facing such an active, in-your-face, hit-'em-with-everything-you've-got opponent.

We won that election. And more than a few people were surprised when I eventually hired Tracy Mehan as director of the Department of Natural Resources. Even though he had helped mastermind, or at least carry out, many of the biting attacks against me, I still felt he was the best person for the job.

Abraham Lincoln said the best thing you can do with an enemy is to make him your friend. He was right. Both the former state senator and the opposing campaign manager have become appreciated allies and valuable friends.

CREATIVE SELF-DOUBT

There's another lesson in this. My father's example showed me that creative self-doubt is one of the most valuable dispositions a person can have. Instead of taking offense and making an enemy, my father took a step back, tried to understand the other party's position, and then, more often than not, chose to give him or her the benefit of the doubt.

When people have honest questions about where I stand or what I'm doing—in politics, this is a daily occurrence—I've learned not to take it as an affront. In fact, when I slow down, I often find that their concerns mirror some reservations I might have on my own. Their honesty, rather than offending me, helps me clarify the situation.

While I believe in absolutes, there are many times where honest, well-meaning people can disagree. How we handle these situations will reveal a lot about our character. Nobody wins when we hold grudges.

I remember one occasion when a state employee and members of the press worked together to create a scandal where there was none. As governor I had plenty of decisions to make and more than enough responsibilities to occupy my time, and this pseudo-scandal became a significant drain. As question after question came up, I found myself thinking some very unchristian thoughts about the person involved. "I don't know when," I said to myself, "and I don't know how, but some day she will remember what she did to me, and it won't be pleasant for her."

Shortly thereafter, we were having our usual devotional time in my office before the workday began. That's a dangerous thing to do if you're holding a grudge. Scripture—particularly the words of Christ—can be brutally honest. Our reading happened to be from Jesus' Sermon on the Mount: "For if you forgive men their trespasses, your heavenly Father will also forgive you. But if you do not forgive men their trespasses, neither will your Father forgive your trespasses."[1]

It was a good reminder for me to reevaluate my grudge, and I asked myself, "Why in the world would you let some little incident like this eat away at your life?" By focusing on it, I had made it worse. By forgiving the persons who were involved in this, I could move on and let it go.

My relief was immense. I could not imagine that such a small burden had become so heavy until I let it go.

Bitterness is a spiritual cancer. That's why I would rather have people be angry with me than for me to be angry with them. Life is too short to spend precious hours fretting about a past wrong. My father's refusal to ruminate on the hurts in his life taught me that relationships are too meaningful to destroy over a perceived slight. What we *don't* say often says as much about our character as what we do say.

C H A P T E R

Six

THE SOUND OF SILENCE

*G*ranted, the 1997 race for the House of Representatives seat from New Mexico was not the biggest race of the year. The election would determine who would replace Bill Richardson, a Democrat who had just been appointed ambassador to the United Nations.

Even so, my friend Ron was eager to follow its outcome. Voters had a clear choice in this heavily Democratic district. Eric Serna, a Democrat with deep roots in the Hispanic community, was a "green" candidate, a darling of the environmental liberals. Running against him was Bill Redmond, a conservative Christian minister and Republican.

My friend woke up the morning after the election and turned on the radio.

Nothing.

He opened up the newspaper, scanning the pages for news of the results.

Zip.

He flipped on the television, scanned CNN and the headline news.

Nada.

Smiling, he turned to his wife. "Good news!" he said.

"What?"

"Redmond must have won. Nobody's covering the story."

He was right, of course. Redmond had won. A conservative winning over a safely held Democratic seat in a minority district is news any way you cut it. But when the media gatekeepers perceive an event as "bad news," they may bury it alive. They can't kill it, but they do their best to hide it.

By learning from what my father *didn't* say, I've also learned to perceive the truth from what other people don't say. It strikes me that our silences are a profound act of communication.

"I GAVE MY WORD"

Until 1997 Michael Jordan, indisputably the leading player in the NBA for over a decade, was never the highest-paid player. When asked why he did not do what so many other players do—hold out on their contracts until they get more money—Michael replied, "I have always honored my word. I went for security. I had six-year contracts and I always honored them. People said I was underpaid, but when I signed on the dotted line, I gave my word."

Three years later, after several highly visible players reneged on their contracts, a reporter asked Michael once again about being underpaid, and he explained that if his kids saw their dad breaking a promise, how could he continue training them to keep their word?

By not asking for a contract renegotiation, Michael Jordan spoke volumes to his children. He told them, "You stand by your word, even when that might go against you." His silence became a roar.

When Dad did not gossip about his superiors, he taught me nobility in the face of adversity. When Jordan did not break his word in order to receive the big bucks, he taught his kids honesty in the face of an industry known for its greed and lack of loyalty.

When it comes to the government, I sometimes wish a little *more* silence would prevail.

THE CHOCOLATE POLICE

It was the holiday season and the government was messing up my fun. No, I wasn't speeding and I wasn't breaking any laws. But there it was, the federal government, sitting on top of my box of chocolates.

I suppose there is a place for nutritional labeling, but I did not open my box of chocolates to be nourished. I opened them because of the way the chocolate melts in my mouth. I opened them because of the heavenly texture of caramel. I opened them because dark chocolate is the most satisfying way to end a holiday meal.

Guess what I learned from the food police? That these delicious chocolates were mostly sugar and fat. That they contained essentially zero protein and dietary fiber. Vitamins A and C? Nope. Calcium and iron? Even considering the heavy calories involved, not much of either.

Calories per three-piece serving (as if I were about to stop at three!)? About 200.

To which I said, "So what!" and wadded up the label with glee.

Do the food police think Americans buy candy for the protein? As Winston Churchill said in a somewhat different context: "What kind of people do they take us for?"

What's next from the Nanny state? Televised messages that sitting on the sofa is not as healthy as jogging? Government warnings that Cheetos do not qualify as a vegetable?

Nobody eats candy to build muscles.

Sometimes I wish the food police would desist and let me eat my chocolates in peace. In this instance, silence really is golden, as it is in yet another situation.

HERE COMES THE JUDGE

I have a favorite question for judiciary candidates when they come up before the Senate Judiciary Committee: "Does the legislature only express the will of the public when it acts?"

The reason I believe this question is so important reaches back to my belief in the communication of silence. The courts sometimes use what they call the "intent of the legislature" as a means of interpreting the will of Congress. This allows them to create new laws simply by asserting that "while the law does not specifically say this, the legislature probably intended to say this."

Some activist judges refuse to accept the inactivity of the legislature or the silence of the framers of the Constitution as evidence that the ignored issues should not be addressed or were purposely not covered by the law or Constitution. Instead they insist on creating laws and constitutional rights where there are none.

What these activist judges fail to see is that where the Constitution is silent, that silence expresses the will of the people. It is preposterous to suggest that the "intent" of those who wrote the Bill of Rights was to force the American public to offer salacious porn to their soldiers. The courts have no business telling the public that they are constitutionally required to use taxpayer money to make pornography available for sale, but that's exactly what happened after Congress passed legislation removing the sale of pornographic material from military bases.

It does not take an Einstein to know that we've had a serious problem with gender relations in the military the past few years. Selling pornographic material on bases only adds fuel to that supercharged, combustible environment, and the Senate, acting on behalf of the American people, believed it should be stopped.

There is no mention in the Constitution, of course, that the military is required to sell pornography. Military stores cannot possibly stock everything available for sale; like any store, they have to make choices. They don't carry every Christian book that's published, for instance, nor do they carry every Christian magazine, but activist judges stepped in and virtually *required* our military stores to carry smut.

Silence is not a vacuum that activist judges need to fill; it's a public consensus that the courts should accept. When the laws and the Constitution are silent, it could very well be that the people are saying, "We do not want government involved here." There are some judges who need to learn that there is communication in the absence of activity.

Yet there are occasions when silence sends a negative message. Just ask the St. Louis police department.

"I'M SORRY"

Each year thousands of prank phone calls tie up the resources of the emergency 911 system. Most of these calls are from children eager to test the system and perhaps insensitive to the consequences of signaling an emergency when there is none.

One day, as his mother took a nap in the next room, eight-year-old Lloyd Rush tiptoed to the phone and dialed 911. When police called back to check out the emergency request, Lloyd's mother, Bianca, took the call.

She was not pleased.

In addition to being punished, Lloyd's mother made him write a letter of apology to the St. Louis police department. Neatly printed in pencil, the note read in part, "I hope you accept my apology. I got a punishment for this. I hope it didn't cause any trouble for anyone."

The police officers were stunned. Though the 911 system is seventeen years old, Lloyd was the first person ever to apologize for misusing it.

Bianca was not the first mother to learn that her son had abused the system, but she was, apparently, the first one to take action. Her refusal to remain silent or to allow her son to remain silent was a thunderous blast to the officials in St. Louis—and an effective message to her son.

How often does our silence tell our kids, wittingly or unwittingly, that what they have done is really okay? What kind of messages are we sending when we choose *not* to say anything at a time when words need to be spoken?

When a dad encourages his son to practice free throws but never mentions the importance of prayer or Bible study, what is he telling his son about what's really important in life? When a mother tells her daughter to dress nicely in clean clothes but never addresses the importance of modesty or unselfishness, what message is she sending? When parents stress the importance of earning a good income but never mention the needs of the poor, what kind of priorities are they helping their children establish?

In parenting, athletics, business, the church, and in government, our silence communicates; it expresses the values we assume and it reflects what we don't think is important enough to talk about. What my father said and didn't say, what my father did and didn't do, what he explicitly uttered and what he felt was not worth talking about, had a profound impact on me.

Based on what you *don't* say, what conclusions might your children or friends be drawing?

Seven

THE HEART
OF THE MATTER

*K*ids often like to test their dads, and I was no different. "Dad," I asked one day, "what would you say if I told you I wanted to marry a black woman?"

My father paused and looked at me with a sincere smile. Then he deftly turned the issue from race, which to him was not worthy of contention, to the issue of faith, which he thought was most important.

"John, what would be trouble," he said, "was if you married someone who didn't share your faith."

This was my father's way of telling me that what really mattered was not skin color but the condition of a person's heart. In many ways, my father urged us to look beyond the superficial and focus on the spiritual, and for Dad, race did not deserve our focus.

From the time I was a young boy, I can remember my father listening to black preachers and black gospel music. This was in the '50s, and gospel radio was virtually nonexistent, but my father searched the dial and often fell asleep to the sounds of black choirs re-creating a hymn, or Reverend Cobb, from the First Church of Deliverance in Chicago, enthusiastically preaching on a passage of Scripture.

One of our family's greatest joys was listening to our collections of Mahalia Jackson's gospel renditions, including her gospel concert at the Newport Jazz Festival. Mahalia's song "Didn't It Rain" is one of the most vital songs ever recorded on American soil.

In my early teens, my father asked me to read *Black Boy* by Richard Wright. It was pretty tough stuff for the mid-'50s, but my father thought it was the best way for me to begin to understand the plight of young black men. While my father certainly did not subscribe to everything Wright advocated, he wanted me to develop a broader understanding of black culture.

Dad particularly liked a book entitled *God's Trombones* by the famous poet James Weldon Johnson. I have always liked the opening line of one of those poems, "The Creation": "And God stepped out on space . . ."

Another poem uses the impact of words to build momentum and meaning:

O Lord, we come this morning
Knee-bowed and body-bent . . .
Lord—ride by this morning—
Mount your milk-white horse . . .

Some of the lines contain a sharp and shocking bit of wisdom:

Young man—
Young man—
Your arm's too short to box with God.[2]

Some might ask why my father bothered introducing me to this culture. After all, there weren't many black families in Springfield, Missouri, from the '40s to the '60s. In my high school, I can remember only a few black students, but I'll tell you this: if you were black, you were as welcome at our house as if you were white. My parents made no distinction. One of my good friends visited my parents and saw a black man raking leaves in the backyard.

"Who's the guy in the backyard?" my friend asked my mom. "Did you hire someone to do some work?"

"No, no, he's a visitor from Africa!" she said. "But he's staying here and volunteered. After three days I let guests help out with the chores just like anybody else."

Visitors were treated like family. We did not have a large house with guest quarters. If you stayed in my parents' home, you sat in the same living room, and ate at the same table; there was no place to hide, and color made no difference.

It did not pass my notice that this was not true everywhere in our country. At the time, there was a major struggle among white people in America who, when faced with a choice about believing the best or worst about black people, all too frequently believed the worst. My father wanted me to know that black people had the capacity to produce things of value.

"Every race has its bad elements," my father told me, "but here's the difference. When white people think about white people, they don't think about the worst white people in the world. When it comes to black people, however, what too often gets talked about are the worst elements."

In other words, he wanted to empty me of prejudice by helping me to fall in love with the highest levels of black performance—and we're not talking athletics here. We're talking literature and the arts, and the gospel treasures that mattered most to my father.

Nothing was more important to my father than his faith, so when I found him listening to black preachers, that told me my father was eager to sit at the feet of black people and learn.

Today that doesn't sound like much. Forty years ago, it planted a valuable seed.

In fact, it was one of the most vivid indicators to me of the difference faith can make. A man who has the foresight to prevent his son's prejudices at an early age is a man who is set on doing the work of God.

LATE NIGHTS WITH REVEREND COBB

During my law school days I felt most like my father's son when I tuned in to WCFL in Chicago from eleven to twelve o'clock at night. For an entire hour I listened to the mellow, wise words of that same Reverend Cobb, who challenged, inspired, and directed me. So much of what he said reminded me of my father, and I began to discover that my father had been shaped by others, just as I was being shaped by him. A wise dad not only serves as a good role model, he gives his sons other role models to aspire to as well.

Reverend Cobb was one of the best. In fact, it may have been from Reverend Cobb that my father learned how to handle bitterness, which I talked about earlier. A familiar refrain from Cobb's teaching was, "It doesn't matter what you think about me; what matters is what I think about you." He went on to explain that we can choose to destroy our spirits by thinking bad thoughts about others, or we can choose to build a spirit of grace and gratitude by thinking good thoughts about others. We can't do anything about what others think of us, so we should simply forget about it.

Reverend Cobb found a way to fit this message into virtually every sermon. "It doesn't matter what you think about me," he'd shout, his voice a wonderful, gravelly baritone, "what matters is what I think about you."

It was the type of thing I'd stay up late to hear, even though I was challenged by the load of law school.

Thus it was natural for me occassionally to visit a black church when I worked in an Anchorage, Alaska, construction yard during the summer to put myself through law school in the mid-'60s. In between loading trucks, keeping inventory, and running a forklift, my spirit would be encouraged by the music and songs that have become such a treasured part of our nation. A shared heritage of gospel music cross-fertilized itself among early white Pentecostals and black churches; hearing that music made me feel right at home.

I cannot tell you what a blessing it was to have a father who was so forward-looking. In the '50s and '60s, some elements in our nation were not so eager to embrace those unlike themselves. Jackie Robinson was still a relatively young man—he did not break major-league baseball's color barrier until 1947—and some people continued to talk openly about segregating our-selves from each other, thereby impoverishing us all.

I'm grateful that my spirit was often lifted through the music of Mahalia Jackson and the Wings Over Jordan choir. My father did not want us just to accept those of other races; he wanted us to respect them and learn from them.

Listening to the God who created all men—red, yellow, black, and white—my father urged me to cherish all those whom God created. He wooed me with the honey melodies of Mahalia Jackson, the fiery insight of Reverend Cobb, and the poetic beauty of James Weldon Johnson. Once you have tasted a cul-ture's highest and best, you are pointed toward respect rather than prejudice.

CHAPTER Eight

PUTTING IT OFF
TO PUT IT ON

My father was a chair gripper. That's shorthand for refusing novocaine in the dentist's office.

Imagine a dentist's drill whirring just inches from your ear. You clutch the chair and brace yourself for what's coming. As the drill bites into your tooth, you feel the searing, penetrating pain, every movement, every bit of pressure.

Tooth dust flies, and you feel it hit your cheek. The drill burns out heat, and you taste it on your tongue. You experience 100 percent of every dig and prod and pick.

Undergoing dental work without novocaine seems Olympian, somewhere on the level of a four-minute mile or a quadruple axel. But my father was a guy who had this "triumph of will over the physical" attitude. When he was diagnosed as a diabetic in his mid-sixties, immediately and with what to me looked like astonishing discipline, he embraced a spartan diet and regimen. Though the diabetes contributed to my father's ultimate heart failure, in another sense it may have actually prolonged his life, because his doctor's prescribed strategy whipped my father into the best shape of his life.

This ability to take the tough road, to put off pleasure for something else, was my dad's North Star of navigation. My father did not make a lot of mistakes in life, but those few he did succumb to made big impressions on him. He dropped out of high school to begin preaching, something he came to question profoundly. He was not sorry about entering the ministry, but he thought it was a serious error not to complete your education in a timely manner.

Because of this, he drilled into us that it was essential to put off some favored activities in order to prepare for a more solid future. As a result, I never doubted that I needed to finish school before even thinking about marriage. Hollywood likes to showcase the tyranny of romantic infatuation—how two people might abandon their friends, family, and beliefs all in the name of an overpowering emotion—but my father just didn't raise me that way. He wasn't a stoic; he didn't despise emotion. But he believed that delayed gratification was an essential practice for success in life. I can remember his wisdom: "John, whatever you do, don't jeopardize the future because of the past."

As one who runs for political office, I have learned to appreciate my father's foresight. There are men living today who probably could have been elected president of the United States, but their extracurricular activities got in the way. And though in more recent times some of these controversial individuals have been elected to national office, their ability to govern has been compromised because of the deadweight of scandals that hang around their necks.

Delayed gratification—putting something off so that you can experience something even better in the future—is a lifestyle that my father believed enriched all areas of life. He expected I would be a father myself some day, and the best way for me to teach my children sexual purity was to guard against premarital sexual activity myself and thus teach by example.

Regarding finances, I learned that you need to delay or even avoid certain expenditures, depending on your cash flow. I don't care how many "toys" you have; if you are deeply in debt, the pressure of possessing those things will bury you a hundred times before they will make you happy.

In matters of faith, my father also taught the importance of delayed gratification. I heard him preach many profound truths of Scripture, but few affected me more than his razor-sharp focus on eternity. One verse always intrigued me: "Blessed are you when they revile and persecute you, and say all kinds of evil against you falsely for My sake. Rejoice and be exceedingly glad, for great is your reward in heaven."[3]

The whole idea of faith includes understanding that the verdict of eternity stands above the verdict of history. I do not think it is possible to live a very sincere Christian life if you lose sight of the power of delayed gratification.

So in my vocational career, my family, my finances, and my faith, my father ingrained in me the principle of delayed gratification: "Don't jeopardize the future because of the past."

THE COST OF GIVING IN

Our government needs to learn this lesson of delayed gratification. With every interest group climbing Capitol Hill to demand a share of the taxpayers' money, Congress has an extremely difficult time delaying gratification. Even though we are still running stunning deficits, Congress just cannot seem to stop spending. Why? We have not learned the secret of saving for something so we can pay cash instead of buying on credit, or saying no to some good opportunities so we can fully fund the best and most appropriate activities.

When we consume now and expect the next generation to pay off the debt, we are limiting the potential of our children. My dad's life was spent living lessons before his children that would *expand* our potential.

If the government were to stop its borrowing, interest rates would drastically decline and the rest of us would save big: over two thousand dollars a year on a seventy-five-thousand-dollar home loan; over one thousand dollars on a four-year car loan; and nearly two thousand dollars on an average student loan.

The power of delayed gratification relates to virtually every segment of human experience. Like anyone else, I struggle with the lure of instant gratification. In fact, I face it every night when, more often than not, I cave in to the tantalizing allure of a hot fudge sundae. I know that hot fudge sundaes are not going to help me live longer. I know I will not be healthier if I add on another five or ten pounds—but those sundaes taste good!

Yet on many a night, I will think back to my father gripping that old dentist chair, the drill whining near his ear, his knuckles white with their clutching. I cannot imagine ever doing that, but I can occasionally put one less scoop of ice cream in my bowl and remember that the best things really do come to those who wait.

Nine

LOVE LIFE

$\mathcal{T}$he first time I saw my wife, she was diligently seated before a law textbook. Both of us were students at the University of Chicago School of Law, and Janet had that wholesome, attractive midwestern look about her that caught my eye. There was an inherent modesty in the way she dressed and carried herself, and she exuded a sense of hard work and confidence by the way she applied herself to her studies. Of course, as a young man it did not pass my notice that she was in the beauty queen category.

After a few days of observation from a distance—implementing my father's concept of delayed gratification—I decided I wanted to get to know her.

In spite of the fact that out of 150 students only a dozen or so were female, I approached her inordinately confident that she would want to go out with me. After all, I was a second-year student, and she was just a first.

On the day I decided to give it a try, I waited at the library, near the desk where she usually studied. After she sat down and organized her things, I tossed my spiral notebook down on the table in front of her.

She jumped.

"Hi, Janet," I said. "I'm John Ashcroft. How about going out with me this weekend?"

She glanced up at me with a slightly quizzical look. I wasn't sure if she was amused, annoyed, or just being polite. "I'm sorry, I have dates this weekend."

I hadn't expected this!

Janet was not going out with just any stranger in Chicago who walked up and asked her.

I walked her to class several times over the next few days so the "we're not acquainted" excuse would no longer apply. I still might be strange, but at least I would no longer be a stranger!

"Well, how about next Saturday?" I asked after we had begun to know each other.

"I think I have a date then too."

This is where my student-lawyer's cross-examination techniques came in handy. "Wait a minute," I replied, "you either have one or you don't have one. You don't just think you have one."

Part of the reason I have such fond feelings toward the University of Chicago School of Law is because that's where I met

Janet. If my father had not taught me to delay gratification, who knows if I would ever have been able to attend law school? And even if I would have been able to, who knows if I still would have been single when I first saw Janet?

Certainly I would not have found someone as wonderful and brilliant as Janet. This is not just a proud husband's hyperbole, by the way. Janet graduated from college with distinction, a mathematics major. And when she went to law school, she did not fool around. Though she was a full year behind me, she took advantage of summer studies and graduated in the same calendar year I did. She now teaches as a university professor and writes textbooks.

When I thus found the woman I knew I wanted to spend the rest of my life with, I was in a position to act on it. My father's teachings had taken hold, and I was largely debt-free when I graduated from law school at twenty-five.

But there was something I needed to check out first. I never wanted to live in town. One of the characteristics I love about my home state, Missouri, is its beautiful country places. We may not have the Rocky Mountains framing our towns, or an ocean lining our border, but there is a peacefulness about Missouri that you just don't see in many other states. It's comfortable, and I like comfortable.

My father had helped me locate a small farm thirteen miles

from where I had been offered a teaching position at Southwest Missouri State College. Part of my father's advice was to settle somewhere so I could trade my property in for something even nicer later on as values went up.

Buying the farm required intense financial discipline, but this stairstep approach worked well in the '60s; it was certainly a wiser move than stretching too far, overextending myself on credit. The house did not have central heating, and an occasional knothole in the floor gave unintended visual access to the crawl space. But the little rock bungalow did have a well and a barn and a fireplace.

With everything thus committed, I was finally able to ask Janet to marry me, but—putting my legal training to good use again—I included an exceptions clause: "Janet," I asked, "will you marry me *and live on this farm?*"

I asked Janet this question as we sat on a gravel bar on the south side of the river located just a stone's throw from the house where we now live. I had tied the engagement ring—I guess I was pretty confident—into the strings of my boots. Hearing Janet say yes on the riverside and farm I had come to love so much was just about the happiest moment of my life. We were able to enter marriage with our professional training completed and a homestead we owned, even if it required us to pinch every penny twice.

I am not boasting about this; I attribute the fact that I was able to enjoy such a strong start directly to my father's upbringing. A solid beginning was his gift to me, and anything I have built on top of that still looks back to the foundation that my father laid—a foundation for which I will be eternally grateful.

In many ways Dad carefully reviewed his own life and thought of pitfalls he could help me avoid. Instead of growing bitter and despondent over tough times, he put his energy into steering his boys through those very same challenges with a lifetime of hindsight and experience.

But there was another element to delayed gratification, an element that would become particularly important *after* marriage—something my father emphasized, "displaced" gratification. That's where we put the needs of others above our own.

BANKRUPT IN LOVE

After a couple of weary hours on the road, my friend Gary Thomas and I pulled over, hoping some greasy food would significantly aggravate our abdomens, at least enough to keep us awake. It has been a lifelong practice of mine to go to some of the worst restaurants imaginable in hopes that the inevitable abdominal distress that followed would preclude nodding off behind the wheel.

The tattoo-laden "fry chef" was having a slow night and

assaulted us with a question. "Tell me," he said, "is it true that your sex life gets better after you're married?"

I choked and stammered. "Uh, mine sure did," I answered, given the fact that I didn't *have* a sex life before marriage.

Then, in an apparent attempt to destroy his employer's customer base, he added an even more offensive comment. "It can be tough being single," he said. "I'll tell you one thing, I'm not getting any tonight."

This young man is an unfortunate example of what is increasingly true about our society in the waning years of the twentieth century: our culture is affluent in sex but bankrupt in love. Ten miles down the road, midway through burger number two, it dawned on me that I should have told this young man, "I don't have a sex life. I have a love life, of which sex plays an important but private role."

A prostitute has a sex life; a porn star has a sex life; even animals can have a sex life. But a married person has a *love life*.

The young man's statement, "I'm not getting any tonight," reveals the orientation of a sex life, not a love life. A love life calls you to focus on giving, not on getting.

Learning to put the needs of others above your own is the "displaced gratification" my father taught me about. The ultimate understanding of displaced gratification is reflected in the life of Christ, who gave up heaven for earth, who could have been crowned king, and who could have called ten thousand angels to rescue Him from the cross. Instead He accepted brutal, humiliating torture on our behalf. He put serving others ahead of serving His own needs.

In delayed gratification, we put off something so that we can enjoy something even better later on—avoiding a "sex life" before marriage, for instance, so that we can more fully enter into the deeper love of the marital union. In displaced gratification, we put off something so that the gratification can go *to somebody else.* Within marriage, for example, we put our spouse's needs ahead of our own.

Displaced gratification is the oil that keeps our society running smoothly. When William Booth finally left the Salvation Army, he sent a one-word telegram to every member of his army. That one word embodied the guiding principle of Booth's life: "Others."

The man or woman who understands delayed and displaced gratification realizes that "others" are what it's all about. Instead of demanding our rights and satisfaction, we can work for the rights of others, we can find fulfillment in seeing other people satisfied, and we can serve instead of trying to conquer.

My father taught me the power of delayed gratification so that I was in a position to buy a farm when I was only twenty-five. Then he showed me the principle of displaced gratification when he actually gave me the choice of two farms to buy. I'll explain this in the next chapter.

Ten

CONSIDERING ALL
THE OPTIONS

$\mathcal{M}$y father made it a point to know his boys. One of the things he knew about me was that I am a country boy at heart; I did not want to live in the city. He came up with a great idea during my last year of law school. "Why don't we send a letter to all the Realtors," he suggested, "listing everything you want, and see what they come up with?"

The idea was to live life with your head up, as in the game of basketball. A good ballplayer has to keep his eyes open over the entire court. You cannot make the best decision until you know all the options before you.

Dad and I drew up our dream property: forty acres, some open land, some woods, maybe water nearby. One of the Realtors came up with a forty-eight-acre property—no river, but a pond and spring, from which the house's water came. (I was always intrigued by that spring, because you could walk down to it and see the intake for the house's drinking water, and right in front of that intake you could watch an occasional frog or snake swim by. Even so, the water was perfectly drinkable.)

I had not yet graduated from law school, but my father walked over the property and thought it looked good, so he put down five hundred dollars to hold it. The next day another Realtor called with more land. As a courtesy, my father went out to look at it, and the place was just too good to pass up. He decided to put money down on that one too.

"John will want one of them," he reasoned, "and I'll take the other."

In this my father was sort of like Abraham with Lot. He took me out to both places and said, "Choose which one you want. You can buy that one, and I'll take the other one."

I was in heaven, a lifetime early.

My father had done all the work and had contacted the Realtors on my behalf, but an interesting dynamic took place. By helping me consider all the options, he increased his own options. He inadvertently found a place for himself.

And, as a bonus, by giving me the choice he ended up with the farm that turned out to be far more commercially valuable. When I chose the rustic place on the river, that left Dad with the farm in the path of development, so he got the better financial deal.

In a way, this demonstrates the biblical truth that when you help other people, you win. Your benefit is "pressed down, shaken together, and running over"[4]—often in increasing measure.

My father had learned the hard way how to get a second start in life by looking at, and then expanding, his options. How else could a man who left high school end up as a college president? My father did it by setting his resolve and going back to high school at nights, supporting his family during the day. He began picking up the necessary credentials to earn a B.A. and an M.A. and then he completed his course work for a Ph.D. at New York University (though he stopped short of doing a dissertation).

A weaker man might have looked at his situation—a wife and kids to support, meager resources—and thrown up his hands. Not my dad. If you wanted something, you looked at all your options, and then you took it one step farther. You figured out ways to expand them. It was a two-part test. I learned that the right result comes first from *working hard to make the right decision,* and then *working even harder to make the decision right.*

This has been an incredibly valuable lesson for me to learn. In raising our own children, Janet and I have tried to help them position themselves so they have a broader array of options. Here is what we have learned together: When you get education, you create new opportunities. When you stop investing in education and start spending on things, you narrow your options. A college degree can catapult you from the crowd; a mortgage will tie you down.

Our daughter asked me what she needed to get out of college. I told her, "Learn a language of the Atlantic and of the Pacific." Our world is growing ever smaller, and the ability to communicate with foreign countries is becoming almost as important as being able to communicate with your next-door neighbor. Consequently, our daughter studied both Spanish and Japanese; having them in her arsenal gives her much broader options.

Volunteering for new experiences can also create new options. Carol Martino of Flanagan, Illinois, just wanted to get out of the house, so she volunteered as a teacher's aide for abused and neglected children. The teacher with whom she worked marveled at Carol's ability to boost kids' self-esteem, and Carol left the school every day feeling so positive she thought she would "explode with goodness."

At the age of forty-six, Carol decided to return to school to earn a teaching degree. She looked at her options, expanded those options, and then created a better life.

The perilous pace of today's society will ultimately require more and more people to make the same kind of changes that Carol made. People are going to have to learn the science of living life heads-up, being sensitive to all the options on the court.

BASKETBALL LIVING

American football is a deliberate sport. I cut my teeth on it and didn't give it up until I left it for rugby in law school. In football there are predetermined plays, and after each play there is a specific halt. On more than one occasion, that stop in the action allowed me to gather my wits and wind. There are real advantages when players get to catch their breath, line up all over again, and get a fresh start. Too often life does not accord us football's stop-action luxury.

In generations past, you could do very well living life as if it were a football game, counting on lifesaving interruptions. That is not true anymore. Life moves too quickly, circumstances change constantly, and what worked in one decade may fail miserably in another.

Years ago, for example, if you got a job with a major corporation like IBM, you pretty much figured you would be there for life. IBM had never laid off a worker, and as long as you performed at a reasonable level, your financial situation was secure. When IBM had its first massive layoffs, almost everyone on

Wall Street realized that American business had entered a new epoch. Few graduating seniors today can expect a lifetime of work for the same company.

Basketball, the science of Michael Jordan, is a much more fluid sport than football. The game of hoops is constantly unfolding, changing moment by moment through a flow of unique, never-to-be-repeated exercises of skill and judgment. The ball can change hands in a split second—a steal, a quick rebound, an unusually fast throw-in after a basket has been made. To paraphrase a comment about politics, basketball is a sport of the quick and the dead—you're either quick, or you're dead. Keeping your head up is not an option; it's a necessity.

One of my favorite basketball players was Pistol Pete Maravich. He did more with perhaps less than anybody in the history of the sport. Jordan is supremely gifted; Maravich was certainly less so. In fact, after Pete died doctors were shocked to discover that he had been living with a seriously deformed heart. He made up for that crippled heart with a panoramic, Argus-eyed vision.

A wide-angled vision is the key to great basketball. You need to use the whole court, and in order to use the whole court, you have to be able to see the whole court. You can't consider all the options if you don't see all the options. Pete saw things nobody else did. It was as if he were playing on a court two times larger than the court anyone else played on.

Pete was also a great innovator. He was never restrained by what had been done before. He perfected behind-the-back passes, and he took the full-court pass to a new level. You never knew if he would pass or shoot behind his head or even make the play milliseconds before landing out-of-bounds in a spectator's lap.

I want my children to have Pistol Pete Maravich's vision in their approach to life. A player you fail to see is a player to whom you cannot make a brilliant pass. An opponent who slips past your sight may very well be the opponent who steals the ball. I want my children to keep their heads up, never lose sight of what's happening anywhere on the court, and thereby create more options for themselves. Basketball gives new meaning to the proverb, "Where there is no vision, the people perish."[5]

In a "basketball life" you learn to spread the defense, find the open spaces, and create a lane to the basket—even under intense opposition. I'll bet you remember one spectacular playoff move by Michael Jordan. The defender was making a brilliant effort. He had Jordan's right hand boxed in, and it looked as though there was no way for Michael to avoid being stuffed. *Not so!* In midair, Jordan switched the ball to his left hand. Score!

When you see all your options, when you're ready to move instantly in response to the changing circumstances, then you're on your way to the winner's circle. You can find new solutions to perplexing problems. That's what the military did to take care of its bird strikes.

BYE, BYE, BLACKBIRD

Jet fighters collide with birds over 2,300 times each year. Military pilots call these collisions "bird strikes," and the damages cost taxpayers nearly twenty million dollars annually.

Scott Air Force Base had a bigger bird problem than most. Its proximity to the Mississippi River made it a popular stop for migrating waterfowl. Blackbirds and starlings were regulars too. At times the control tower had to stop landings and take-offs because of "severe bird conditions."

The Air Force tried everything—cannons, lights, and alarms, to name a few—but the enemy refused to budge. What they really needed was a more sophisticated weapon.

And they found it.

The Air Force finally turned to one of nature's more frightening natural predators: the peregrine falcon. When trained falcons were released on the airstrip, the other birds flew for cover the same way little kids fly for recess—fast. According to the handler's stopwatch, an intimidating falcon could clear an airstrip of birds in as little as six seconds.

Some people who have noble aspirations fail on the first or second try and think they're stuck. Usually a solution is there. We simply have to consider a broader set of options. When we do, even one thought to be "for the birds" can become a highflier.

Interestingly enough, more and more football teams are switching to a "basketball" philosophy, a more fluid style of play that can react more quickly to changing circumstances. The famed West Coast Offense calls on players to run various routes, depending on the defenses they encounter as the play unfolds. This strategy wins by adapting and changing rather than trying to force old options—square pegs—into new circumstances—round holes.

I have seen too many people compromise their way into misery and dissatisfaction. They did not look at other options; they took the first road that presented itself, and they plowed ahead into a quagmire.

Today's graduating seniors will go through six different *career* changes. Not just a company change, but a career change. If you are an educated person who has learned how to learn, you can adapt, make new plans, and set new ideas into motion, even when you are boxed in by the perfect defense.

This is why I believe we generally ought to reserve federally funded job training for those who have completed high school or their GED. These basic educational skills enable workers to adapt and meet the needs of ever-changing technology.

My own career has required constant adaptation. Even after

the people of Missouri reelected me as governor by the highest margin since the Civil War, term limits prevented a possible third term and redirected my career. I lost a subsequent race to become chairman of the Republican National Committee. It shook my confidence. Sure, losses had hit me before, but that was back when I was paying my dues. Now I was used to winning. I needed a new strategy.

The adaptable basketball approach to life is liberating, because it means that your life is not something that happens to you. You and your character happen to it.

I once heard a preacher say that circumstances do not determine character, they *reveal* it. I was reminded of this truth in a particularly poignant way in the summer of 1996.

"GOD IS GOOD . . ."

A man and his wife maneuvered a wheelchair through the thick crowd at a large outdoor festival in St. Louis. A tall boy, secured with straps and braces, sat in the chair. His parents showed considerable dexterity, simultaneously carrying their dinner, pushing that chair, and enjoying a beautiful summer day.

Up close you could notice the father's bright purple shirt. In bold letters it read, "GOD IS GOOD . . ." The three dots let you know there was more to the message on the back, so after he walked by many turned to read the rest of the message: ". . . ALL THE TIME."

What a tremendous philosophy of life! What a powerful shield with which to face another difficult day.

God is good, all the time . . . even when your son is strapped into a wheelchair.

God is good, all the time, even when you lose your job.

God is good, all the time, even when the Dow drops or the crime rate rises or church membership does nothing more than merely stay the same.

God is good, all the time.

I will not forget the courage, confidence, and faith of this man, eager to proclaim his belief that God is good, all the time. This is a man who does not sit off in a corner, licking his wounds, asking the entire world to feel sorry for him: "I can't enjoy the festival because my son is in a wheelchair."

Real character is not shown when everything is going your way; it is demonstrated when you are left alone, when a sudden shock has cheated you out of the resources on which you have come to depend, when unexpected adversities present themselves with a malicious ferocity, and you're living on the edge of fear and faith. Character is what you're made of when everything that might hold you up evaporates on the spot.

Even if you have made a few wrong decisions, by carefully considering all the options you can create new opportunities. The techno-saturated future we live in demands that we raise children who are willing to try new things, learn new lessons, and come up with new solutions.

When Michael Jordan is in midair, Phil Jackson can't coach him. Those famed Nike shoes can't deliver him. It's just Michael Jordan, one-on-one with the defender. Somehow he's got to get the ball out of his hand and into that hoop. That's when greatness is revealed. I call it the basketball approach to life.

Eleven

HATS, BATS, AND THE INTERNET

$\mathcal{A}$long historic Washington Avenue in downtown St. Louis, Paul Schneider and his brother, John, have been making hats for seventy-five years. Their handmade creations have been worn by a Who's Who of world-famous people, including several first ladies.

Though the women's hat business has waxed and waned in popularity, the Schneiders, now in their nineties, trace their most challenging moment in business to Vatican II.

Vatican II? Why?

Vatican II updated the worship service of the Roman Catholic Church. As part of that, the pope decreed that it was no longer necessary for women to wear hats in church. The hat business took a tailspin.

The Schneider brothers put their custom-made thinking

caps on and managed to make the necessary adjustments. They increased their market in other areas and learned to make hats that were not targeted primarily toward the Sunday morning crowd. Several decades later, the "open" sign on their store proves that business is as strong as ever.

If we want to live life for the long haul and stay in business longer than two to three years, we need to learn the Schneiders' ability to adapt to changing times. As these brothers approach their hundredth birthdays, they are still able to gauge what is fashionable. These resilient American entrepreneurs deserve our respect and admiration. As a matter of fact, my hat's off to them! They have discovered the basketball approach to life. So has Kenneth Rutledge.

BATS

Kenneth did not care much for school. Math, English, geography—none of those subjects held his interest as much as did four bases and a pitching mound. Resolved to become a big leaguer, Ken did what he had to do to get to the next grade but nothing more. He was going to be a ballplayer; why did he need to study math?

Kenneth Rutledge received what he calls a "blank diploma" from high school, then joined the St. Louis Browns baseball team. He was a remarkable player . . . until the day his pitching arm gave out.

What do you do when you put all your eggs in one basket and fate scrambles them up?

If you're Ken Rutledge, you make an omelet.

Unemployed, with no hope of returning to baseball, Ken took a minimum-wage job. He had squandered his opportunity to get a formal education, but he figured he could still learn.

After dinner each night the television stayed cold and the radio stayed silent as Ken began reading books on business. He could scarcely afford to buy a paperback, much less a hardback, but the library offered a borrower's card at exactly the right price—free.

Ken and his wife settled into a comfortable routine. He stayed up late reading books, and she got up early to return them the next morning and to check out new ones. Ken's "self-education" continued for many years.

The reading paid off, and Ken stair-stepped his way to the rank of vice president with a Fortune 500 company. Ironically, those who were not familiar with his past assumed he was a highly educated man. He was clearly an expert in management and labor negotiations, and other executives in St. Louis regularly sought out his counsel. After Ken's retirement many executives sent their children to him for business advice.

When fellow executives respect you enough to entrust their children's future to you, you know you've achieved something special. Today Ken tells those kids how important a good education is. To those who approach him after having made a few mistakes, Ken might say, along with Pastor Buntain, "IT'S NEVER TOO LATE TO START OVER AGAIN," and "IT'S ALWAYS TOO SOON TO QUIT." He might not mouth those exact words, but if you watched as closely as you listened, you would come to that exact conclusion.

An adaptable spirit can do more than launch a new career. In Serbia, it helped to launch a revolution.

THE INTERNET

Serbian dictator Slobodan Milosevic must hate progress. I'm sure he longs for the good old days when tyrants could rule in peace. Now there's this pesky little thing called the Internet.

As soon as Milosevic realized that the municipal elections were going against his party, the Serbian dictator ordered the nation's last vestige of the free media—an independent radio station—to leave the air.

That would have worked fifteen years ago, but today Milosevic is living in a different world. No sooner was the gag order issued than tens of thousands of students, professors, professional people, and journalists rushed to the Internet to link up with web sites carrying news on Serbia's crisis.

The independent radio station simply converted its

newscasts into a digital format and put them out over audio links to the Internet. Milosevic and his thugs quickly realized their error and backed off. Maybe the radio wasn't so scary, considering the alternative. Even though they continued to try other means of repression, the bullies have not found a way to silence the thunderous roar of freedom represented by the World Wide Web.

The secret faxing of banned documents played a legendary role in the fall of the Soviet Union. A home page may have saved a revolution in Serbia. We have seen the beginning of the partnership of information technology and democracy, but it is *only* the beginning. The rules are changing for everyone.

When my father was born, commercial air travel was the stuff of science fiction. Two years after he died, we landed a video-transmitting probe on Mars. We and our children must learn to adapt, to consider all the options, and—where we run up against the perfect defense—to create new options. Earthly tyrants as well as spiritual tyrants (such as defeatism, lethargy, and self-pity) cannot keep down an innovator with faith and vision.

CHAPTER
Twelve

FEEDING THE SOUL

T woke up knowing one of two things: either I was going to have a full-time commitment for at least the next six years, or I was going to be a man in need of a job.

It was voting day, and my name was on the ballot as a candidate for the United States Senate.

Early that morning, as dawn broke over the hills, I sat at the piano—not unlike my father during my childhood—and found myself singing:

> *Keep me true, Lord Jesus, keep me true.*
> *Keep me true, Lord Jesus, keep me true.*
> *There's a race that I must run, there are victories to be won.*
> *Give me power every hour to be true.*

It took me a moment to realize what I had just sung—

"There's a race that I must run, there are victories to be won"—
and I smiled. Maybe the tiny hymn would prove prophetic!
That song stayed with me throughout the day, becoming a heartfelt prayer.

I cannot imagine a day without music. Sometimes it's hard
to imagine going sixty minutes without at least one song running through my head. I think I inherited this from my dad, as
he was one of the biggest music fans I've ever known. If an
instrument could be plucked or blown, my father had probably played it. He was at his best on the piano, trumpet, and
trombone, but he had flirted with the violin and cello as well.

Sometimes his affinity for picking up an instrument could
be unnerving. On one occasion, Dad was invited to a professor's house for dinner. The professor brought out a mandolin
and exclaimed, "Hey, I bought this thing called a mandolin,
and I'm learning to play it. Listen."

He plucked a few strains of single notes, got caught here
and there, and had to go back, but my father identified the tune.

"Let me see that thing," Dad said.

The professor handed Dad his mandolin and my father
plucked the strings cautiously. He slowly played his way through
the scales, then repeated them more quickly.

"I think I've got it," he said. "This is kind of like a violin."
Then he set off on the strings of that mandolin like he had been

born to play it. The prof looked apoplectic; he had spent months trying to learn an instrument that Dad rambled over in minutes.

The professor's wife, sensing trouble brewing, broke into the living room with a loud voice. "Dinner's ready!"

That incident, revealing Dad's facility with a new instrument, showed me clearly the unique nature of Dad's musical talent and understanding. As a young preacher, Dad rode his trombone around the world as he played his horn in his ministry.

A lecture might inform someone, but music affects us in a far more profound way. Music can go past the intellect to the intimate, moving us so compellingly, we are different for having encountered the enriching blend of notes, tones, and ideas.

Music has fed the soul of our nation almost from its beginning. A favorite, true story of mine is the tale of a music-loving pastor who literally shot hymns at the British during the Revolutionary War.

As the Redcoats advanced toward the Elizabeth Town Presbyterian church in New Jersey, Pastor Cauldwell noticed that our troops were desperately low on wadding for their muskets. Without wadding, the muzzle loaders could not fire, and the music of religious liberty and a free nation might not be heard from Boston to New York, much less from sea to shining sea. Racing into the church, Cauldwell began tearing pages out of hymnals, including a special favorite, "The Old One Hundred"—Isaac Watts's rendition of the One-hundredth Psalm.

Charging back into the thick of the fight, the pastor ran from man to man, stuffing hymnal pages into their pockets, shouting, "Give 'em Watts, boys, give 'em Watts!"

Music has found its way into most American wars, from "Yankee Doodle," "The Star-Spangled Banner," and "The Battle Hymn of the Republic" to the World War melodies of this century. But I doubt music ever had a more practical impact and effect than when it came out of the business end of the muzzle loaders defending Reverend Cauldwell's Presbyterian church.

In our own personal "battles," there is nothing like music to keep us inspired and to strengthen weary hearts. If you have an important business meeting, a tense moment with an unruly teen, a relational or personal challenge, you can hardly do your soul any better than to nourish it with some good music.

Music can also be one of the best bonds for a lasting friendship, such as my relationship with Judge Max Bacon.

"OR WAS THAT STATE PEN?"

Max Bacon and I sang together for well over twenty years. One time we were invited to sing at a church, but somebody had printed the wrong date in the bulletin. We showed up at the right time, in a sanctuary that had room for three to four hundred people, and were greeted by two elderly women!

Max and I looked at each other, smiled, and decided to give these ladies a full concert. They enthusiastically clapped their hands between songs and we had fun saying things like, "Thank you, *both of you,* thank you very much."

It was fun singing with Max because he has such a great sense of humor. He teased me unmercifully, chortling that a politician's insistence that there was a "public outcry" for him to run for office meant that his mother and father thought it might be a good idea. When a politician cited "a veritable groundswell" of support, that meant his aunt and uncle agreed with his parents.

On another occasion Max told a crowd that he loved singing with me. "John and I have sung all over the country," he said. "We've sung in great churches, and on college campuses, even at Penn State . . . or was that State Pen?" The truth is that we *had* sung at the state pen.

Music was the introduction and cement to my friendship with Max, and music has introduced me to other relationships as well. Senator Trent Lott, the Senate majority leader, would not normally spend a couple of hours a week with a freshman senator, but my participation in The Singing Senators has opened the doors for us to get together on a regular basis to practice. Together with Idaho's Larry Craig and Vermont's

Jim Jeffords, we have now sung in more than ten states, including California, Texas, New York, Vermont, and North Carolina.

The physical and spiritual benefits of actually creating music can be energizing, like the chemical endorphins the body releases after running or eating. This is a radically different dynamic from simply observing a musical performance.

For me, singing can even curtail seasickness. It happened when I was shark fishing between Huntington Beach and Catalina, off the California coast. Pitching to and fro in the dead of night has a way of making you feel absolutely insignificant and puny.

The Pacific chop was tossing us unmercifully, more than our little twenty-two-footer could absorb. It passed the rolling motion on to our stomachs, and I began to feel queasy.

Of course, it did not help much that we were fishing for sharks. The best way to attract sharks is to buy a bucket of fish entrails at a bait store and hang it over the side, leaving a slick of fish slime to attract the prey.

Just as queasy was developing into an overboard experience, I began singing, "It Is Well with My Soul." (Trust me: this hymn was chosen by faith, not immediate experience.) I could particularly relate to the line "When sorrows like sea billows roll . . ."

After just one or two stanzas, I was amazed by the way

singing stabilized my insides into a manageable calm. We stayed out on that water for several more hours, continuing to attract sharks with the slick of fish slime alone.

LITERATURE

Next to music, my father loved literature. If music feeds the soul, poetry nurtures it. My father was actually an amateur poet. He loved literature and taught his boys to memorize great works of poetry, sometimes bribing us with a buck so that we would have the initial motivation to embark on a literary voyage.

Many times, as I have faced struggles, these poems have come back to my mind, bringing me a lift. One of my favorites is by Edgar A. Guest, entitled "It Couldn't Be Done":

> *Somebody said that it couldn't be done,*
> *But he with a chuckle replied,*
> *That maybe it couldn't, but he would be one*
> *Who wouldn't say so till he'd tried.*
> *So he buckled right in with a trace of a grin*
> *On his face. If he worried he hid it.*
> *He started to sing as he tackled the thing*
> *That couldn't be done and he did it.*
> *Somebody scoffed: "Oh you'll never do that;*
> *At least no one ever has done it";*

But he took off his coat and he took off his hat
And the first thing we knew he'd begun it.
With a lift of his chin and a bit of a grin,
Without any doubting or quiddit,
He started to sing as he tackled the thing
That couldn't be done, and he did it.
There are thousands to tell you it cannot be done,
There are thousands to prophesy failure;
There are thousands to point out to you one by one,
The dangers that wait to assail you;
But just buckle in with a bit of a grin,
Just take off your coat and go to it;
Just start to sing as you tackle the thing
That cannot be done, and you'll do it.

Dad taught me that there is nothing like music and literature to nurture the soul as we pursue noble aspirations.

CHAPTER
Thirteen

THE TRUE
PORTRAIT OF LOVE

I was twelve years old and sure I'd never live to be thirteen. All I had was a bad case of the stomach flu, but when you're twelve, agony quickly personifies itself as death. The flu rivets your attention until the entire world's existence can be summed up as one violent and nauseous stomach. You can't imagine ever being well when you're feeling that horrible.

As I sensed another eruption, I ran to the bathroom, my mother following behind me. During healthier times, we kids would find creative ways to describe throwing up: barking at the ants, yawning in technicolor, that kind of thing. Now it was no laughing matter. I knelt over the bowl and prepared to upchuck. Just as I was certain I would throw up not just my lunch but my lungs, kidneys, and liver as well, I felt my mother's gentle but firm hand sustaining my head. She literally held up my head as I emptied the contents of my stomach into that toilet bowl, an act that even today amazes me with its selfless and tender devotion.

I would have done anything to avoid that situation myself; I was practically praying for an out-of-body experience. But here was my mother, who did not have to go through this, not only standing by me but holding my head with those chore-cracked hands.

My mother was the type of person who would give up a pleasant afternoon to walk the halls of a hospital or nursing home, finding someone to comfort, talk to, and pray for. But during my first term as governor, the tables were turned when my mother was diagnosed with cancer.

As my mother entered the world of the dying, my father's love for her became far more apparent than before. Dad was not perfect; he had been so focused on other things and ministries throughout his life that, though his love for my mother was apparent, his profoundly felt passion lay partially hidden behind a list of things to do. Once he realized that his remaining time with my mother could now be measured on a few calendar pages, he became inordinately attentive, with a gentle, detailed kindness we had never witnessed before.

POETIC CARE

My mother's imminent passing was a particularly bitter pill in that she had only recently returned to Missouri. My father's work had pulled her away from her children as she followed Dad around the country, but my parents came back during my first year as governor. As a son, I could not have been more delighted, but within weeks that joy was marred by the sobering diagnosis that her cancer had become aggressive.

We were faced with an awful decision, the same dilemma confronting so many families: do nothing and watch the cancer steadily march its assault on life, or try another round of chemotherapy—an arduous road of suffering and internal trauma—in the hope that this chemical war would kill the disease without killing my mother.

Mother courageously chose chemotherapy, and it killed her. It was an awfully high—and ultimately futile—price to pay for hope. In her last days, the drugs so blistered the inside of her body, I began regularly swabbing out her mouth to assuage that terrible reaction to the chemistry.

Standing at the bedside of a sick loved one provides ample opportunity for serious reflection. And it is a sobering moment for any man when the years collapse on themselves and the son begins parenting his mother. I would soon lift her coffin with a bewildering array of emotion. This was the woman who had "carried" me into the world, who had fed me as an infant, whose arms had held me and lifted me as a child, and now, here I was, carrying her to her final resting place in the earth.

I think some Jewish funerals have it right in this regard, with the friends and family who are gathered around the grave being the first ones to throw dirt onto the coffin. And friends and family—not strangers—should be the ones who usher us into the new experiences to which God has appointed us, especially death.

As I regularly checked my mother's condition at her bedside, it occurred to me that there are few more powerful acts of intimacy than helping people die the way they ought to die. I am not, of course, talking about the perverse acts of a Dr. Kevorkian and so-called "assisted suicide"; but there is transcending value in accepting the personal burden of helping loved ones make their destined crossing into eternity. We do not "push" them into eternity—the question of when they take that final step is God's alone—but it is an honor to be there to hold their hands and help them remain connected to what matters most until those things are taken from them by God's design and they fully enter the realm of the spirit—and the eternal realities that indeed matter most.

Weeks before I had gone to my mother as she grew sicker and tried in vain to get her to see that this might not really be the end. She looked at me with tired eyes and in a weary voice said, "John, it's not necessary for you to say things like that. The Bible tells us there's a time for living and a time for dying. The time for dying has come."

I bit my lip and tried to deny it, shaking my head, but she wouldn't have it. Some people who are standing on the edge of eternity know exactly where they are. Trying to argue with them is an exercise in futility. They see something we don't. When godly persons die slowly, they seem to wade into eternity rather than dive into it, remaining only partially on this earth with one foot already in heaven.

My mother slid into a coma several days before she died. Our family vigils around her bedside were seasoned with Scripture, silence, and song. They were beautiful, yet fearful moments. The beauty was in remembering and honoring a woman who had given us so much. The horror was in watching this precious woman succumb to the assault of sickness and then death. Both realities came together in a startling way when my mother chose to grace us with one final act.

LAST MESSAGE

As we sang for my comatose mother, I could get no assurance that she even knew we were there. Her expression remained placid and distant, perhaps even a little hollow. The moment I knew we had broken through came not from looking at my mother, but from watching my father. His stoic face twisted with a strange compassion and utter agony. I looked down to see its source. A single crystal tear on my mother's sunken face slipped out of her eye and gently washed down her cheek, hitting me like a tidal wave. Just a tear, but it bowled me over. She was still there, and she still cared.

That was the last message my mother ever gave us, the last communication between my father and the woman he had loved so much—a woman with whom he had shared his life. In my father's sigh I heard the depth of what a lifelong love can be, a love of the spirit that can find a seventy- or even eighty-year-old face more beautiful than the flawless skin of a young, blushing bride. I saw in his eyes an adoration that surpasses any silly notion of love at first sight.

I looked down at the telltale trail of the tear that had escaped from my mom's soul, and I looked up at my elderly dad scratching out a gospel tune, half-choked with emotion, watching his wife die. And in that picture, I saw the true portrait of love.

Fourteen

THE POSITION'S THE THING

—————

*W*e're so glad to have Senator John Ashcroft with us today," the emcee said. "Please help me welcome Senator John Ashcroft."

As if tethered to the same puppeteer, the entire room rose for a standing ovation, and I waved them down. "As a politician, it always strikes a bit of terror in your heart to be greeted by a standing ovation," I admitted. "All too frequently, people use it as a cover to slip out unnoticed, so I'm thanking you not just for standing up, but for sitting right back down."

The occasion reminded me of the story of a congressman greeted by a thunderous ovation. He stood and basked in the applause, until a bold but rather small, elderly woman cried out, "Not me! Not me! Not me!"

Everybody was stunned and grew silent as the woman cried

out for all to hear, "I wouldn't vote for you if you were St. Peter himself!"

The congressman was sharp, responding, "Lady, if I were St. Peter, you wouldn't be living in my district."

Only two things are said about people in public life: their enemies make disparaging comments that are too bad about them, and their friends offer compliments that are too good. If the politician believes either one, he's in trouble.

My houses are filled with plaques, honorary pictures, honorary keys, and other tools of recognition given to me while I was a governor and now a senator. But these are temporary acknowledgments of an office I held, not indications of the man I am or hope to be.

You begin to learn that many institutions will use plaques and degrees as a way of getting you to their events; it's not necessarily to commend your performance, it's often about their need to get the press there for a good photo opportunity.

I'm not ungrateful for honorary degrees, but I want a balanced understanding of who I really am, and I do not want to participate in some sort of delusion that I'm something I'm not.

Two thousand years ago a rich young man came up to Jesus and began a question, "Good Teacher, . . ."

Before Jesus answered the question, He queried, "Why do you call Me good? No one is good but One, that is, God."[6]

Jesus would not let the young man flatter Him, though in His case, flattery was probably impossible. Think about it: virtually any positive remark you could make about Jesus would be true! Even so, Jesus did not look to others to validate His worth, and neither should we.

That's why I do not focus on what is written about me in the newspapers, either the "too-good" or the "too-bad." I do not want to measure my life by what people are saying about me.

My father drilled into me the fact that genuine self-esteem finds its source in the virtue of God, not in the praise of men; it's based on what God thinks of you, not how many stand in line to shake your hand or slap you on the back.

I try to adopt a forward-looking approach, focusing on what I might become in the future, not on what others are saying about me today.

THE QUEST TO BE REMEMBERED

As a two-term governor and senator, people often ask me, "How do you want to go down in history?"

I respond, "I think you may be making a faulty assumption."

"What's that?"

"That I'll be known or remembered at all."

The fact is, I probably won't be. That's hard for people to see when my name persistently pops up in the morning papers and on the nightly news, but the same thing was true for senators and governors fifty years ago, and precious few of us can name even one or two of them now.

Sometimes I'll add, "The verdict of history is inconsequential; the verdict of eternity is what counts."

It's a political fact of life that if your friends win all the elections following you, you will be better known, well regarded, and well understood. If not, you'd better look out. History is written by the winners, and they often stake their claim by inflating the accomplishments of their friends and denying the merits of their opponents.

It is gruesome to watch so-called modern "historians" distort and invent facts to project the promiscuity, immorality, and inconsistency of today's culture on the principled patriots of colonial America. One can only wonder if they simply cannot tolerate a good example. Too many historians have taken Mark Twain's comical quip, "There's nothing so disgusting as a good example," and turned it into a mission statement.

Thomas West has written an important book, *Vindicating the Founders,* in which he demonstrates convincingly the Founding Fathers' integrity and philosophical consistency.

These were not perfect men, but they were by and large good men of integrity, far removed from the shallow, duplicitous, self-centered hedonists that so many modern "historians" make them out to be.

History will always be written with bias, but the judgment that really matters will not be entered here. Our bosses might underestimate us; our families might underappreciate us; but the judgment we really ought to shoot for, the one that counts most, is being written in the heavens. God keeps the eternal record.

ATTITUDE OF GRATITUDE

Our search for fame and self-esteem can be an exhausting one. My father insisted that his kids look past it. He forbade us to use the phrase, "I'm proud of . . ."

"Say you're grateful for it," my father suggested. "Not proud."

He had an acute awareness that so much of what we enjoy has been *given* to us and can be traced back to the benevolence of God. In my father's house, Thanksgiving was the biggest holiday of the year. It was also his favorite.

When we are grateful rather than proud, we avoid the haughty spirit that often looks down on others who perhaps have not done so well. It also allows us to *enjoy* God's blessings rather than defending them as if our identity and self-worth are dependent on them. Unfortunately, what we have can so easily be taken from us in a sudden, life-changing moment.

My father knew this by personal experience. When Dad was a young boy, a neighbor woman, distraught that her pipes had frozen, called my grandfather to ask for his help.

My grandfather asked for some kerosene to use in thawing the pipes, but he received gasoline instead. In the cramped crawl space of the house, the gas exploded violently, burning my grandfather severely. Disabled, he could no longer work; and without his railroad check, he had no income.

They would not let my dad even see his father at the hospital, but after much pleading, some nurses finally agreed to wheel my grandfather to the top of the stairs. My dad, a young boy at the time, waited eagerly, but his mouth dropped open when he saw a mummy-wrapped figure, with holes cut out for eyes and mouth.

"That's not my father," he said. "I don't know who it is, but that's not my father."

Christopher Reeve was a successful, relatively wealthy actor with a bright future. One fateful jump with a horse and he became a quadriplegic. A happy family, a healthy body, a good income—none of these are guaranteed absolutes. They should not be points of pride but reasons for gratitude. Our self-esteem should not be based on externals, because we have no certainty that they will remain.

Without an attitude of gratitude, we cannot fully appreciate the unique nature of God revealed by Christ. The pagan gods required the sacrifice of human beings. In centuries past many devout pagans delivered their daughters to a watery grave or sacrificed their sons on cruel and fiery altars.

Our God does not ask us to sacrifice our children for Him. Instead, He sacrificed His Son for us. Pride does not fit here. Gratitude is the only appropriate response.

Our self-esteem comes from understanding that God values us enough to redeem us, not that we are valuable enough to redeem ourselves. If I wake up in good health, my family protected, my job intact, my financial portfolio secure, the only appropriate response is gratitude. And at the end of my life, what matters most will not be whether I warrant a footnote in some historian's tirade, but whether the God who blessed me on earth will remember my name in heaven, giving me the ultimate validation: "Well done, thou good and faithful servant."

CHAPTER

Fifteen

THE NATURAL ORDER

$\mathcal{I}$ was hoping to say hello. All morning long I was thinking of things to tell him, hoping for a day at the lake with my
younger brother, Wes. When he did not show up, I gave him a
call to see if he was coming or if something was holding him up.

The phone kept ringing.

Maybe he's on his way, I thought, so I plodded around the
house, puttering away the time. When I heard tires crunching
the gravel in our driveway, I walked eagerly toward the door,
but I felt a chill when I saw it was Hilker, from my governor's
security detail.

Hilker's arrival was an extraordinary gesture. The detail had
my number at the lake, so they could call me if a state emergency arose. The fact that this man wanted to tell me something
in person immediately signaled to me that something very serious was wrong.

"It's my father, isn't it?" I asked as soon as I opened the door.

"No. It's your brother Wesley."

"Is he hurt?"

"I'm sorry, John. I think it's worse than that."

Numb is the only word that fits. I felt numb, hollow, empty—but mostly just numb.

When I got to the hospital, my brother's wife, Denise, was there. She wanted me to be with her to view the body, so together we walked in and saw the human frame that had once held Wes's soul. His body was still strapped to the tilted table where they had tried unsuccessfully to shock him back to life. The car accident's neck-breaking fury had killed him instantly without leaving a mark.

I reached out and touched his arm. His skin felt stone cold. I had never felt death so tangibly in all my life.

Just a few hours before, this body had held a man in the prime of his life. He had a wife to love, a business to mind, and three young children to support, all of them between the ages of ten and fourteen. Wes had massive physical strength, and he frequently carried up to 280 pounds on his six-foot-two frame. He loved bicycling, usually riding twenty miles a day, and lived an aggressively active life. That's why it was so shocking to see this once-strong Norwegian body lying so passively vacant. The frame that could snatch up a bag of cement with one hand now needed someone to close its eyelids.

The air seemed suddenly thin as Denise and I stumbled out of that emergency room.

INNER RESERVES

I have an unofficial sister, Joy Collins, who has been a part of my family since before I could tie my shoes. The day of my brother's funeral, Joy was on one side of the church and I was on the other as we watched my father look into the open casket that held my brother's body. Dad stood like a man who was valiantly but unsuccessfully fighting despair. Time seemed to slow down when both Joy and I noticed my father beginning to sway in front of the casket.

Joy ran from one side of the church, I rushed from the other, and we managed to reach him just as his knees buckled. My father half-collapsed in our arms.

I had never seen him this way. He was neither a strong nor weak man physically, but his inner reserves were legendary; yet they were failing. At the time, I did not want to admit it, but it seemed that a part of my father was buried in his son's casket.

Six weeks after Wesley's funeral, my father had a massive heart attack.

A BROKEN HEART

The day before, my family had arrived at a ski resort in Colorado, eager to taste, tackle, and terrorize the world's most famous snow. Our skis were waxed, our poles were laid out, and everything was ready for another mountainous assault when I received one of those dreaded, dark-of-night phone calls.

"John, your father's had a heart attack. He's in the hospital, and it looks pretty bad."

I looked at the clock: just after 2 A.M. By four that morning we had every member of the family and every article of clothing back in our van. We drove straight through to Missouri, where I rushed to my father's hospital bedside.

The first pounding strains that exploded my father's heart came at Wes's death, leaving Dad's heart as scarred and torn with emotional grief as it was marked by physical weakness. In fact, I think it's fair to say that my dad, who passed away three years later, ultimately died of a broken heart. He could manage the pain, but he couldn't escape it. It lingered, and it hurt.

GOOD FORTUNE

A wealthy Asian man is said to have commissioned a work of art. He had one aim in mind. "I want the art to represent good fortune," he said. The artist was free to choose painting, sculpture, or any art form at all.

The artist came back with a work of calligraphy, not uncommon in the Far East. It was very beautifully done, with three large and terse statements:

Grandfather Dies

Father Dies

Son Dies

The man who commissioned the work admired its beauty but protested, "This is depressing! How can this possibly represent good fortune? Everyone dies!"

The artist smiled and said, "The good fortune is in the sequence."

There is something profound about this. It reminds me of Jesus' words when He said, "I am in the Father, and the Father in Me."[7] In some spiritual sense, the Son and the Father lived a life that was intertwined. This heavenly truth has been translated to our earthly sphere. It has been echoed by poets through the centuries, including John Donne, who penned these famous lines in 1624:

No man is an island, entire of itself; every man is a piece of the continent, a part of the main. . . . Any man's death diminishes me, because I am involved in mankind; and therefore never send to know for whom the bell tolls; it tolls for thee.

No man or woman dies without affecting another. We are too close for that.

My father's stoicism had always been a part of his character—the chair gripper at the dentist's office. But there was no chair gripping at the time of my brother's death. Dad's reaction revealed to me how deeply our earthly fathers live in us. When we die as earthly sons, part of our fathers die with us; a little bit of the life they passed on to us is wiped from the face of this earth.

This is particularly true if the father and son have an unusually close relationship. Wes lived in the same town as my father, so he would often go by my father's house to visit.

"Wes," my father had said, "you don't have to come by all the time. You can just call me if that's easier on you."

Wes peered at him and said, "Well, Dad, a phone wouldn't work for what I want."

"What's that?"

"Sometimes I just want to lay my eyes on you."

My father relished that phrase. He was not a man who displayed many emotions, but he loved to recount this incident, and the memory of it nourished him in the winter of his life.

Maybe that's why I don't treat my father's failure to recover fully from Wes's death as a sign of weakness but of strength. Dad had so invested himself in the spirit of his son, he could not fully reclaim that investment when his son preceded him in death.

In fact, my father's reaction to Wes's death starkly demonstrated how much my father cared for each of us. Intellectually and theoretically, I knew he loved us, but that's not the same as witnessing the debilitating anguish that collapses a grown man's posture and makes him walk a little less tall. My father's sunken stance became a profound statement of love and affection.

Wes was gone, the natural order was broken, and my father was severely shaken. The season was as dark as it was meaningful. Yet behind my father's eyes you could see the imprint that Wes's life had left behind, buried there in the soul of a man who loved his son more than life.

Yes, Wes was absent. But looking into my father's eyes, I saw he would never be forgotten.

Sixteen

THE STRONG SIDE OF WEAKNESS

---

 ine contestants assembled at the starting line for the hundred-yard dash. At the sound of the gun, they all started out—not in a dash, exactly, but with relish for the race and its challenge.

This was the Special Olympics in Seattle, and no sooner had the race started than one runner stumbled on the asphalt, rolled a couple of times, and began to cry. The rest of the field heard the cry, slowed, and looked back. Then every runner turned around and went back to the fallen boy.

One girl with Down's syndrome bent down to give the boy a kiss. "This will make it better," she said. The boy gamely stood up, then all nine participants linked arms and walked to the finish line together.

The stadium stood and cheered. There had been faster races,

certainly, but none more inspiring. These kids, in their weakness, revealed a transcendent compassion.

It is important for a father not only to pass on his strengths, wisdom, and insight, but also to model how a son should handle weaknesses, failures, and insecurities.

INSECURITIES

My father could have scheduled his life five years in advance with preaching and speaking engagements, if he had wanted to. His was not the flashy fame of a glamorous young evangelist or megachurch pastor. Rather, his renown was built pew by pew and student by student over the breadth of a life well lived.

Yet despite all this, a certain insecurity sometimes invaded his thoughts. I heard him say several times, "You know, John, if I weren't a college president, I wonder if anyone would still care about my thoughts, opinions, or beliefs."

Like so many men, my father struggled with equating his personal value with his credentials and vocational portfolio. Absent his credentials, he worried that the culture would not care about his ideas.

Once weakness is spotted in a person, there is a temptation to devalue him for it. But true relationship comes from discovering weakness as a bond rather than a wall. Instead of saying, "You're weak, therefore I can't love you," we can say, "I love you with your weaknesses." And sometimes we can even say, "I love you because of your weakness."

That last sentence might sound strange, but let me explain. In my father's case, his weakness was a certain insecurity that one day his judgments might not be regarded so highly. If we look at this weakness from another perspective, however, it can actually become a strength that further endears us to him and his ideals.

You see, my father valued wisdom. He valued insight. What he feared losing most was his participation in sharing these godly qualities. He did not fret over his retirement portfolio. He did not openly bemoan the indignities of aging and the loss of strength. Instead, he just wanted to remain active in the dissemination of ideas.

There is beauty in that weakness because it tells me that my father had his priorities straight, even if he allowed a little insecurity to slip inside now and then.

Another weakness of my father was that he was almost hopelessly "prone to belief." Organizations or teachers with this "positive" approach to life were always his favorites. He loved Dale Carnegie and Norman Vincent Peale.

PRONE TO BELIEF

When someone promised my father something, he assumed the person was telling the truth until that person was proven unreliable. Dad was not a cynic or a skeptic. He believed you should interpret everything in the best light rather than the worst, and he paid the price on more than one occasion for this perspective.

I remember one time in particular, when Dad was building a cabin at the Lake of the Ozarks. A contractor pitched a new process for shooting concrete, spraying it to bind blocks together without using mortar. My dad swallowed this hook, line, and sinker, opened his wallet, and bought a mess.

Once again, someone could look at this and say, "Your dad sure was gullible." But I would never want to be raised by a cynic. Believing in the best, hoping for the best, and giving others the benefit of the doubt may not be the most astute financial approach, but it is good spiritual advice. My father may have died with a few less zeros in his bank account because he habitually trusted his fellowman, but his lack of worldly riches was more than made up for by the relationships and respect that sustained him to his dying day.

My dad never pretended he was perfect. He could laugh about his mistakes, and this proved to be a wonderful tonic for our family. I appreciate this, in part because I have seen the damage inflicted on the psyches of men who cannot admit their weaknesses.

A good friend of mine, an accomplished man with a sincere faith, really got himself into trouble when he became dependent on alcohol. As a high-ranking public official, he could not visit a liquor store anonymously, as many do. And because his denomination didn't believe in drinking, he could not risk buying alcohol from a grocery store. Instead, he began doing something very foolish: he started surreptitiously snatching bottles off the local market's shelves, slipping into the men's room, and satisfying his need. Once the bottle was empty, he simply left it behind.

This friend was an accomplished, intelligent man. He probably realized the inevitability that someday the store would catch on and set a trap. But he was consumed with keeping a precarious balance on the tightrope of a hidden habit, and he ignored all the warning signs.

It may be possible to deny one's problems, habits, and dependencies, but the words "you're under arrest" and the papers of prosecution provide an inescapable dose of reality.

Of course, my friend's career was ruined in the short term. He left office disrespected, though he has since courageously and tenaciously recovered and risen to even higher levels of service.

I remember going into his office before his "fall" and seeing pictures of him when he was at his very best. It was an impressive assortment. Every senator would envy some of these shots, with him standing next to the world's highest and mightiest and greatest, the typical "me with____" pictures that cover so many of our walls and offices in Washington, D.C.

These pictures captured a man who was larger than life, and the pressure of my friend to live up to those pictures almost destroyed him. He could not admit his problem when his denomination forbade it. He could not admit his dependency when he lost his control. It took a humiliating public exposure for him to stand up to his weakness.

When people say pictures don't lie, they fail to realize that our favorite pictures attempt to suggest that our very best moments are *persistent* moments, yet they're not. We might have looked like that for a split second, but minutes later our hair moved, our clothes wrinkled, our expressions grew tired, and our faces sagged back to normal.

To keep up with our picture-perfect image, many Americans spend millions of dollars a year on plastic surgery. We create cut-and-paste bodies, dye our hair and bleach our teeth, and spend enormous amounts of time and money trying to rearrange our inevitable middle-age spread, all to cover up who we really are and how we really look.

When I was a boy, I hated to get my picture taken; just hated it. Consequently, early childhood photos reveal a pouting face, my lower lip protruding halfway down my chin. Ironically, I now make my living getting my picture taken. Politicians have a phrase we like to use for the many receiving lines that make up so much of our lives: "Grip and grin." People often apologize when they ask to have their picture taken with me, but I tell them it's the easiest thing I do. Shaking somebody's hand and looking into a friendly camera is a holiday compared to an aggressive news conference.

At these grip-and-grin functions, I occasionally meet Hollywood celebrities. Since I don't watch a lot of movies, sometimes I have to be told who they are; many of them don't look all that special to me. Without the camera lights framing them just perfectly, an international film star may look no more spectacular than a few of my friends from a Sunday school class.

America has had a love affair with glamour for many generations, but my dad had a sense of comfort about who he really was. When Dad sat down and played the piano as he sang, he knew full well he was not Van Cliburn or Pavarotti. Yet all kinds of people reminisce to me about my father's music; not because the music that poured out of him was technically perfect, but because it came straight from his soul.

Some people will not play unless they can be the very best, but I have found that a few weaknesses can actually endear a performer to a crowd. In fact, many of the most popular performers are *not* the best musicians; they have simply learned to connect with the crowd in a special way. Often they use their limitations as a bridge of intimacy rather than a wall of exclusion.

Men who insist on always being "strong," who refuse to show their weaknesses, are men who often selfishly and proudly refuse to serve others by letting themselves be served. Everyone wants to be needed, so when we reach out to another person and say, "I need you," we fill a basic need in that other person's life.

Let's put the picture-perfect photographs in perspective. Let's admit that we need help even if we look good on the outside. When we do this, we do not demean ourselves, we simply value others.

Seventeen

LETTERS

*I*n the spring of 1993, while practicing law in St. Louis, I wrote to my friend Governor George Mickelson of South Dakota to update him on my activities in the private sector.

Just days later, on April 19, the Mitsubishi MU2 twin-prop jet carrying Governor Mickelson worked its way through a violently turbulent spring storm. At 3:55 P.M., it slammed into a concrete silo near Dubuque, Iowa, instantly thrusting my friend into the hereafter. According to the news reports, the plane went down around the same time I was reading George's response to my letter. You won't believe his words: "I practiced law for twenty years before I ran for governor and, with eighteen months to go, am trying to decide on what I might do in the 'hereafter.'"

In an irony of ironies, he may have entered eternity the

moment I was reading those words expressing his concern about the hereafter.

Truth is stranger than fiction. If I ever attempted to write a novel containing this incident, critics would undoubtedly assail the plot as unrealistic and contrived. But this really happened. I know George wrote *hereafter* to refer to his life after he left the governor's mansion, but in light of the plane crash, that choice of words turned out to be tragically poetic.

If, rather than writing back, George had called me on the phone and chatted, "Yeah, John, I find myself thinking about the hereafter these days," it would not have had a fraction of the impact of his letter.

There is a transcendent, persistent, and enduring quality about the written word.

PRECIOUS WRITING

In 1985, while leading a trade mission to the Far East, I penned a letter to my parents commemorating their fiftieth wedding anniversary and thanking them for what they meant to me. If you will indulge me, I would like to share portions of that handwritten letter with you now:

Dear Mom and Dad,
    As I write this from Tokyo it is not yet the eighteenth in

America, so I have the opportunity to be among the very first to (on your day) say *Happy Anniversary!*

More than anything else, gratitude sweeps through me for the life you live together and the godly consequences that flow from it.

Needless to say, without you I would not exist as a human being. Just as important, without you I would not exist as a personality. You shaped me—pushing, guiding, praying, supporting me. Bob and Wes, who have joined in your assistance to me, are your responsibility as well.

When I inventory all of God's goodness to me, I find that yours was the hand He has used over and over again.

Your selfless devotion to the kingdom of God has taught me the most important lesson, that there are more important things than me. It is strange that we only learn of our value as persons when we understand that there are values and missions that transcend our standing as persons. . . .

Each of us, your sons, enjoys the blessing of "intact family" in large measure as a result of your teaching and example. As important, if not more so, are the thousands of others who have learned to cherish your lives as blueprints for service to each other in pursuit of Christ's mission.

Mom and Dad, I love you both beyond description. My prayer is that I may never disappoint you or let you down. I continue to need your prayers and support desperately.

My first five days here in Tokyo were bleak, rain-filled, dark. The eighteenth dawned bright, filled with sunshine. It is a fitting celebration of your marriage and family.

I am not only grateful for you but grateful for this chance to say how grateful I am. Thank you for everything! You have been a part—and are a part—of everything I am or ever will be.

Of all the things I communicated to my mom over forty-five years, I think this letter moved her the most. I know she read and reread it many times before she died a few months later. She even showed it to friends; try doing that with a phone call!

When Mom died, the letter passed on to my father. When Dad died, the letter came back to me. My grandchildren will be able to read the letter after I'm gone. If you really want to "reach out and touch someone," reach for paper and pen, don't dial the phone.

I had plenty of practice writing letters during my first year of college. My dad made a deal with me: "I'll write to you every day that you write to me."

That was all it took. I don't know what he expected—perhaps two or three letters a week for the first month or so, followed by an occasional letter every other week—but I scribbled out at least a short letter every day of my first year in college, even if it was just a twenty-five-word missive before I went to sleep. The reason was simple: if I ever stopped writing, the day might come when I would go out to the mailbox and not have a letter from my dad.

That never happened. My entire freshman year was lived with daily input from my father through his written words.

Later in life my father found more creative ways to get the grandkids to write back: every letter from Grandpa as a follow-up to their letter contained a crisp dollar bill!

WRITE IT DOWN

Our culture has consistently placed a higher value on the written word than the spoken word. A few great speeches—Lincoln's Gettysburg Address or Martin Luther King Jr.'s "I Have a Dream" speech—have achieved a certain measure of fame. But infinitely more people have read these speeches than actually heard them spoken.

If something is really important in our culture, what do we say? "Write it down." When teachers threatened us as school-children, what were the most terrifying words they could utter? "I'll put this in your permanent record!"

If two companies plan to do business, do they settle for a

phone conversation? Absolutely not. They say, "Fax over a contract. If we like it, we'll sign it." Promises that are made in writing are more enforceable in a court of law.

This mystique about the printed word is why some people struggle so mightily to get their names in the paper. A few deranged souls have even succumbed to tragic acts, such as attempted (or successful) assassinations, just to get their names "written in the history books."

All of us seem to have this same fascination with the written word, and my father understood this in an almost prophetic way. There is something about being able to put a letter down and then pick it back up that makes it special. If it's a particularly precious letter, we can read it over and over until we practically know it by heart—but even then, we still read it, because it's more fun to see those words dance off the page than to recall them verbally.

This is especially true if the letter is handwritten. The familiar scrawl of a dear friend or relative carries the mark of a person's being; one look at the handwritten address on the envelope and you instantly know whom the letter is from—and you smile.

Virtually every day of our lives, you and I have a chance to write a letter to someone we deeply care about. Maybe we have struggled sharing our heart when we're face-to-face or speaking over the telephone, so the deliberate pace of writing will allow us to express what we really feel. Or we can simply write a short note to thank someone for a favor or encourage someone who is going through a difficult time. Our letter or note may wind up in a child's scrapbook, a teen's memory box, a parent's cedar chest—or a history book. We never know.

Imagine how your spouse might feel if she woke up tomorrow morning with a short note left on the refrigerator or stuck in her briefcase. Imagine the smile on your daughter's face and the warmth cascading across her heart if she opened up a lunch sack and found that her dad had slipped in a short, two-sentence note: "I love you. I hope you're having a great day." Even twenty-five words, if they're the right ones, can make a difference.

If you have something important to say, take a tip from my father: write it down.

CAPITAL DECISIONS

*A*s history would have it, the practice of executing murderers, which had long been frozen by our judicial system, began to thaw during my first term as Missouri's chief executive. Suddenly the governor's office operated as the final appeal for men on death row, and this created serious pressure on me personally.

Among those sentenced to death was one who had managed to get married during his time on death row. His wife would come to church occasionally, sitting close to me. Once she spoke very briefly to me, but most often I think she just wanted me to sense her presence, perhaps hoping I would somehow respond by pardoning the killer.

And then there were the letters.

You can feel the pressure of a letter written: "Dear Governor, You now hold a man's life in your hands. He has been sentenced to die, but you need to know that he has become a Christian. He is truly repentant and sorry for what he has done, so I'm asking you to commute his death sentence to life in prison. After all, he's not just a criminal—at least, not anymore. He is now a brother in the Lord."

Answering that kind of mail is not easy, but at the risk of sounding flippant or callous, my decision was not quite as tough as it may appear. Let me tell you why.

CHOICES

I remember an old family movie of my father and my older brother, Bob, taken before I was born. When Bob was barely a toddler, Dad set him free in a park with lots of trees and shrubs and things to explore. Bob was off like a flash.

Then my father did a curious thing. As soon as my brother turned his back, Dad hid behind a tree. He stayed out of Bob's sight, though always remaining within a few steps in case there was need for a quick rescue. He wanted my brother to be free to begin making judgments and decisions on his own.

That film vividly captured my father's style of parenting: setting his boys free to explore opportunities, though always being nearby in case his children needed some help.

There is a tremendous difference between command and choice. My father resisted the parental urge to raise children who could respond only to fear, manipulation, or domination. Instead, he raised us to govern ourselves according to the Judeo-Christian principles of the Bible and with an understanding that our choices have consequences.

Many people paralyze themselves trying to figure out the will of God, but Dad taught me that where God's will is clearly laid out in Scripture, we do not have to figure it out; we just have to do it. And in less clear-cut situations, God expects us to use mature reason and judgment, guided by values expressed in His Book and by His Son.

My father's deep respect for personal responsibility mirrors the foundations of our faith. The very nature of our Judeo-Christian culture is choice-driven: "I have set before you life and death, blessing and cursing; therefore choose life, that both you and your descendants may live."[8]

Two distinct voices have rung through the annals of time. The first voice says, "Do whatever you want. It won't make a difference because you're free." The other voice, belonging to God, says, "Choose carefully, because you are meaningful and make a difference."

The voice that said, "You're free," does not describe freedom as much as it describes *meaninglessness.* When Eve heard, "It won't make a difference," what the devil really meant was, "You don't have consequence. You are meaningless."

Because our lives have meaning, there are consequences to our actions, and we must learn to accept them. Our culture is infected with the thought that freedom means the lack of consequence, but the laws of nature and of nature's God know that there are no inconsequential acts—which brings us back to my decision about the man who was sentenced to die.

On the day that any execution was scheduled, I lived with a constant awareness of what was about to take place. I had received the appeals long in advance and had organized teams of attorneys who would send me thick files full of documentation. The attorneys had carefully reviewed the information. I told them to bring to my attention any salient points or any compelling reasons why the judgment of the people of the state should not be carried out.

Even when everything appeared to be in order, I would stay in my office or near a handy telephone in case there was an extraordinary or late-breaking development. This was not likely. Most of the men sentenced to die had been convicted eight to twelve years prior, and their cases had traveled through numerous legal reviews and evaluations at virtually every level of the judicial system.

I had to learn not to assume responsibility that was not mine. My decision was whether to interrupt the process, not whether I would kill. Though that decision is a weighty one, it would be equally sobering to say to the people of Missouri that their system of justice has not worked.

I chose not to commute this man's death sentence. Just because a murderer has learned to love the Lord does not mean the state should pardon him. As a Christian, I am willing to forgive him; but as governor, it would have been inappropriate for me to pardon him unless a mistake had been made in the judicial proceedings.

My guiding philosophy was fairly simple: state law had given me powers as governor for a particular purpose. If the people had somehow convicted someone who did not warrant conviction, I was to step in and correct it. It was *not* my responsibility to second-guess the people; it would have been arrogant and irresponsible for me to commute every death sentence, or the death sentences passed on newly converted Christians, arguing, "The law says this is to happen, but I'm going to replace that law with my own opinion."

I was the ultimate appeal to correct error, not reward regret, emotion, or even religious conversion. Becoming a Christian may remove us from *eternal* penalties, but it does not relieve us or others from the consequences of our acts.

I also gained some insight into this decision-making process through my relationship with President Ronald Reagan.

"THANK YOU FOR SAVING MY LIFE"

Though we were not close friends, Reagan generously traveled to Missouri to help my campaigns in 1974, 1976, and 1978. In fact, his support in 1976 proved decisive; without it, I do not believe I would have won.

When I served as chairman of the National Association of Attorneys General, we had a meeting in Washington, D.C., and several members asked me to arrange a meeting with the president. I was delighted when President Reagan agreed to meet with us. It was a small group, fewer than half a dozen, and as we chatted in the Oval Office, the president raised the issue of capital punishment.

He had faced this dilemma while serving as governor of California, and he recalled the demonstrators who regularly paraded in front of the governor's mansion, and who even, on some occasions, hassled his children. With a slight chuckle, the president mentioned how some Christian ministers began tolling their bells in anticipation of the execution.

"I told them, 'If you'll toll your bells every time somebody is murdered, I won't mind if you do it every time the state executes a killer.'"

The president admitted he found the responsibility somewhat traumatic, but an unexpected package he received gave him a new perspective and a stronger resolve to continue with what he believed was right. After a highly publicized execution, Reagan received a small box in the mail at the governor's mansion. Inside the box was a wood carving, with a handwritten letter that began, "Governor, thanks for saving my life."

The rest of the letter, Reagan recalled, went something like this: "I'm seventy years old and my wife and I run a liquor store. Last week, a thug broke in while we were there. He intended to rob us, but I resisted him. He wrestled me to the floor, and once I was pinned, he poised his knife above my throat. I had both my hands on his wrist, struggling with all my might to keep him from killing me. As I grew weaker and weaker, I finally shouted out, 'Go ahead and kill me! You'll get the death penalty and be executed, just like the guy last week.'"

The letter continued, "He dropped his knife and ran from the store. Thank you, Governor. Your fortitude and resolve saved my life."

There was a moment of silence after the president finished telling this story. We were all lost in our own thoughts until President Reagan finally broke our silence by adding, "In case anybody asks you about my position on capital punishment, you can tell them I favor it; and if they want to know why, you can tell them this story."

In the end, capital punishment saves lives. Even though I believe this, following through was never an easy task.

When I was growing up, I doubt my father ever imagined that his son would become governor and have to decide whether to commute a death sentence. But he prepared me to take on decisions such as these by teaching me to make decisions based on values and consequences.

My children are at the age where their vocational paths are just now becoming apparent. My goal has been to give them what my father gave me: a love and respect for the power of wisdom and the application of time-honored values. Whether they serve as soldiers, engineers, teachers, lawyers, business owners, or entrepreneurs, they will make their own capital decisions—hopefully from a tested frame of biblical values.

Nineteen

LITTLE THINGS
MEAN A LOT

St. Louis's 1997 science fair for children had a remarkable addition: a sophisticated science project that compared the size of dinosaurs to humans. It was a fine project, but what made it even more impressive was the fact that it was the painstaking work of a kindergartner named Stephanie Hulsey.

Stephanie's love of dinosaurs began with dinosaur cards at age two. Since then Stephanie has read and studied everything she can about dinosaurs. (She now reads at a fifth-grade level.)

Obviously, Stephanie did not get where she is without some parental sacrifice. There were a lot of trips to the library. On one occasion Stephanie's mom even contacted a dinosaur model manufacturer to check out inconsistencies her kindergartner had caught! And since young children cannot write well, Mom happily tape-recorded her daughter's narrative for her science project and converted it to a three-ring binder.

What one thing did Stephanie's mom do to raise such a remarkable child? There is no answer for that, because there *wasn't* just one thing. There were a lot of little things—and it's the little things that count.

LITTLE HABITS, BIG IMPRESSION

My father had many habits, which were not cataclysmic in their impact, but which taken together said a lot about the type of man he was. It does not matter how tired we dads are, how unfairly we have been treated, or how grumpy we feel—whatever we say and do will be picked up, recorded, and all too frequently imitated by our children. There are no "time-outs" for fathers.

Adults who are not operating as parents sometimes forget this. When the Franklin family visited the Capitol in the winter of 1998, they were appalled by the everyday workings of the Senate. Like good parents, the Franklins train their three children (from five to thirteen years old) to listen when others are speaking, so imagine their dismay as they sat in the Senate gallery and watched our government at work. As opinions were pontificated, other senators talked. Or read. Or stretched their legs. Or visibly yawned. The senators would have been reprimanded for inattention at the Franklins' dinner table, but here they fit right in while being paid rather handsomely.

The original rules of debate for the Constitutional Convention in 1787 did not allow conversation when another member spoke. No reading of any kind was permitted during debate, and no one was allowed to speak twice unless everyone else had spoken once.

These are just tiny rules, but maybe the breakdown of these little things has led to such low public confidence in Congress. If the proceedings of the Senate do not appear controlled, it's no surprise that we seem powerless to rein in a bloated government and runaway federal spending.

When I was in Sunday school, we used to sing a little song that went something like this:

> *Be careful, little eyes, what you see;*
> *Oh, be careful, little eyes, what you see.*
> *For the Father up above is looking down in love;*
> *So be careful, little eyes, what you see.*

It might be appropriate for us fathers to rephrase that song to read,

> *Be careful, father's eyes, what you see;*
> *Oh, be careful, father's eyes what you see.*

For a little tot you love looks to you up above;
So be careful, father's eyes, what you see.

TWO THINGS

Every day my father did two things; both said a lot about what he valued. First, he had devotions. For him, spiritual preparation was paramount—you begin the day seeking your heavenly Father's presence and blessing.

It's a habit he has passed on to me, one that is particularly hard to break. I saw no need to stop during my two terms as governor or now as a senator; the day does not really start for me until we have had our time of devotions.

The second daily thing my father always did was to shine his shoes. He was fond of admonishing me, "John, dress for the job you want, not the job you have." This was his way of telling me that spiritual preparation should not eclipse physical preparation; the two go hand in hand.

"Can people see you in the job you want?" my father asked me. "If you don't look like you'd fit, they won't consider you when the job becomes open. Prepare yourself and conduct yourself in such a way that you'll seem like the natural choice."

To this end, my father encouraged me to be conservative and professional in my dress. "If you have a sharp white shirt and a tie, you can carry off virtually anything," he insisted, and he was right.

Many of you will remember that back in the '70s men wore all kinds of loud and colorful shirts. I tended to stick with white. When a reporter asked me, the young state auditor, about it, I smiled and said (remembering my father's words), "A white shirt is the mark of a civilized man."

Unfortunately, the governor at the time set a fashion trend against white, favoring blue shirts! Television cameras were not nearly as refined as they are now, and a white shirt could actually wash out a person's face, so the general recommendation was to go with a soft "television blue." But I was not on television, or at least not that often, and my father's preference for white was hard to shake. I had learned to respect the "little things."

Other routine acts of my father added weight to his life and my spiritual inheritance. I never saw my father consume food without bowing his head to pray. I never saw him openly express his anger at my mother in front of his children.

My father was never on time—he was always *early*! In this respect, he lived by the philosophy of Vince Lombardi, whose players created the moniker "Lombardi Time." According to the famed Green Bay Packers coach, "on time" was not an option. Those who did not show up early were labeled late. Dad drilled this habit into us with the intensity of a staff sergeant; the

Ashcrofts were consistently among the first ones to church. On Monday we should be one of the first to show up for work. In Dad's mind, showing up late was just plain sloppy living, and my father did not oblige sloppiness.

Dad did have some small, quirky habits. He loved to drink tea out of bone china teacups because he thought they were particularly elegant. One time he addressed a church in Canada, during which he let slip his affection for bone china cups. That evening he returned to the church and found a box with a label: *To J. Robert Ashcroft.* He opened the box and found a beautiful china teacup.

At the evening service he thanked the person publicly, as no name had been left anywhere on the box. "I don't know who left this cup, but I want to thank you. My wife and I will really enjoy this, and we'll think of all of the new friends we've made here."

The next night he came back to the church and thirteen bone china teacups were waiting for him! (I have inherited some of those cups and this cowboy occasionally enjoys the refinement of decaffeinated tea served in fine china.)

But the biggest thing my father taught me about the little things in life is that the importance of the little things is out of proportion to their size. I have worked hard at remembering this.

A Chinese proverb says that the journey of a thousand miles starts with a single step. Dad did not write proverbs, but if he had, I'm sure one would have been, "A man's character begins with his handshake."

Dad was an enthusiastic hand shaker. He would shake the hand of every person in his office every day. I remember watching him with fascination as he did this. Many people in his position would say, "I'm too busy. I've got too many important things to do. I can't spend time greeting each person. It's just a small thing, anyway. It doesn't really make any difference."

But it does.

As president of several colleges, my dad frequently sponsored events in which my mother and he invited virtually everybody at the college to their home. Some leaders govern by fiat; my dad governed by relationship.

It became clear to me that what my dad was doing was to give everybody standing with the president—and by everybody, I mean *everybody*. Some of the people who came to these receptions surprised the degreed professors. My father was not interested in just getting to know the faculty or even the administrative support personnel. He wanted to relate to the janitors, the groundskeepers, and the cafeteria workers. He valued and recognized the people others thought of as expendable and easily replaceable.

"John," he would say, "when the details fall apart, the entire operation disintegrates," and he was right. A house might be built with large planks of timber, but if you pull the nails out, what will happen?

Because he respected the "little things," my father did not believe that anyone qualified as a "little person." Everyone was important.

I have seen my dad's principle—the importance of the little things is out of proportion to their size—work for so many others.

BIG CITY, LITTLE THINGS

Ask yourself what you would have done if you had inherited New York City five or ten years ago. Crime was out of control and more than half of the citizens admitted in a survey that they would move out if they could afford to. The city was a depressing place, and it must have been a somewhat daunting job to be elected mayor.

Where do you start?

Mayor Rudolph Giuliani started by going after the little things. "I am a firm believer in the theory that 'minor' crimes and 'quality of life' offenses are all part of the larger picture," he explains.[9] Among the first elements to go were the "Squeegee Men," drug-addicted and shady-looking riffraff who personified New York's rough edge. Armed with a soiled rag and a dirty bottle of watered-down Windex, these men would bully and badger motorists for money.

Giuliani said, "We're not going to put up with this anymore," and he brought this intimidation to an end. He then declared war on graffiti, subway panhandlers, loitering, broken windows, and petty vandalism—minor offenses that would have gone unnoticed in days past while the police force was overwhelmed with homicides and violent crime. But Giuliani had a hunch: if you send out a signal that you won't tolerate these minor offenses, people will get the idea that the major offenses will be treated even more seriously.

"One graffiti defacement or one loud radio may not seem like much of a problem, but criminals thrive in chaotic environments," Giuliani explained. "Small problems can be the first step to big trouble. Neighborhoods scarred by graffiti or blasted day and night by boom-box radios will become besieged, vulnerable, and ultimately dangerous places. If police departments surrender on the small issues—using the excuse that they are too busy dealing with 'serious' crime—they soon will find themselves surrendering to the latter as well."[10]

It worked. Giuliani has been successful in reducing crime beyond all expectations. Between 1993 and 1996, the murder rate came down almost 50 percent. Robberies plummeted by 42 percent while auto thefts dropped by 46 percent. The streets of New York City became safe in a way that was unimaginable just a few years earlier.

Oftentimes as parents we get "stuck" or lost in the big challenges of life. *What can I do to really get through to my kids?* we wonder, but the truth is if you take care of the little things, the big things will fall into place.

In a family, in a business, in a school—yes, even in big cities—it's all the same: the importance of the little things outweighs their size.

Twenty

BUY A DOG

---

*M*y father did not leave behind a sizable financial portfolio. He wrote a few books, but none of them are still in print. He did not have a lot of collectibles. No schools are named after him, no foundations set up to pass along his assets.

The reason for this is simple: my father put his stock in relationships. To him, people mattered most, because only people have eternal significance. He understood the truth behind Walt Whitman's words: "The genius of the United States is not best or most in its executives or legislatures, nor in its ambassadors or authors or colleges, or churches, or parlors, nor even in its newspapers or inventors, but always most in the common people."

My father threw his energy into building friends, and the spiritual capital this produced was nothing short of overwhelming.

I live in continual amazement that wherever I go in this country people come up to me and mention a special memory of my father. He freely entered their lives and left behind a rich heritage of fellowship I am still reaping today.

My father made it clear that once you establish your vertical relationship with God, the next step to a meaningful life is investing wisely at the horizontal level, mining the rich quarry of personal relationships with friends and family.

The most meaningful relationships are the ones that have survived the precarious passage of mutually shared risks.

RISK

My Senate schedule gives me precious little time and very few options to move our bass boat from the farm to the launch site, and from the launch site to our cabin dock. I cannot usually afford to wait for pleasant weather, so on one ominous day, I asked my friend Smitty to help me get our boat in the water so it could be used at a later date by my son Jay.

The radio reports as we trailered the boat to the launch presaged violent spring weather, the credibility of which were reinforced by intermittent hail. The frozen kernels rattled the roof of my old Ford van like shotgun pellets. I began to wonder whether this trip would be wasted.

God appeared to be blessing our endeavors, however; the storm abated once we arrived at the launch site. Darkness had come early and the late sun had succumbed to the dense clouds, but we decided to go for it. After all, the hail had stopped, and it was only four miles from the launch to our cabin.

The boat had barely gotten wet when the fury of the storm reminded us that the rain falls on the just as well as the unjust. I looked at Smitty, who was hunkered down behind the console, and said, "No rain is gonna stop two tough cowboys like us."

He winced a positive nod.

Then all hail broke loose! I'm not talking sleet. I'm not talking BBs. This stuff made mothballs look like kid's play, and it made total wimps out of two would-be cowboys. We turned tail and sped for the cover of a vacant dock. Later that night, the National Weather Service pinpointed a tornado within spitting distance of our position. The way we see it, we didn't get spat upon; we got tidal-waved.

I have taken my boat up the lake hundreds of times, in weather as unremarkable as it was benign. But there is something unforgettable about that trip that Smitty and I will carry as part of our friendship for the rest of our lives. Yes, it was a humiliating drenching and an altogether ill-advised run, but it was also the kind of shared, survived risk that cements friendships.

Too many of us live on the surface of relationships without ever diving into where it really counts. People who will join us in our vulnerability are our true friends; people who want to join us solely in our assets are our associates. Harry Truman once said, "If you want a friend in Washington, buy a dog." I've heard many a congressman similarly lament, "Since I've arrived in Washington, I have a lot of associates, but I'm not sure I have any friends."

One of the problems of public life is that when you are in a position to do things that people consider to be beneficial, they will befriend you; but they won't necessarily *be your friend.* There is a major difference between these two realities. Unfortunately, you can never really know where you stand with someone until your capacity to benefit that person is gone. That may sound like a jaundiced view, but it's all too true.

When I served as the state auditor of Missouri, I had prime seats—located near the center of the action—for all university football games. After I lost the race to be elected to that post, I not only lost those prime seats, I occasionally found it tough getting into the stadium!

Men and women who pour all their energy into a position or vocation instead of relationships are setting themselves up for a debilitating depression when that position or vocation is taken away from them. That's why one of the things I'm most thankful for is that my father taught me the value of true friendships.

Twenty-one

MORE IMPORTANT THINGS THAN ME

———

ew things are more eternal on this earth than a young boy playing baseball. Inning after inning, the entire universe is reduced to a dusty diamond and your best buddies. Even forty-five years later, I can still remember many of the guys on my team—Alan Hale, Bobby Adams, and Roger Talbot, to name a few. The leather gloves, the duck-billed hats, the stitched balls, the Louisville Sluggers: these are the gateways to the heroic game played by the Babe, the Iron Man, Mickey, and Stan the Man.

Standing above it all is the man who controls the most important thing in the world—the batting lineup. When you bat, whether you bat, and what position you play are determined solely by a man who will forever be known as your coach. If he lives to be ninety-five years old and can barely get out of bed, you will still call him "Coach." He earned that right, decades ago, when he entered the hallowed sanctuary called Little League.

I played baseball for Coach Wilcox. His friends called him Charlie; we just called him Coach. His son, Kirby, was on our team. Kirby was a hard-throwing outfielder who, just a decade or so later, would make the ultimate sacrifice on the fields of Vietnam.

Before every game and many practices, I would catch sight of dads earnestly giving their sons the last-minute tip: "You gotta choke up on that bat, son; it's getting away from you." "Swing earlier, boy; hit that ball in front of the plate." "I want you to pick up a little dirt with that ball, Tommy; the cardinal sin at shortstop is letting a ball go under you."

After those final pieces of advice, the heavyset umpire finally called out the glorious words, "Play ball!" The fathers slapped their sons on the shoulder or fanny, then took their places in the bleachers, occasionally talking to one another, maybe shaking one of the other dad's hands if his son made an unusually good play.

After one particularly hot day of baseball practice, Coach Wilcox took us kids up to the root beer stand, near what is now the Glen Isle Center in Springfield. He walked up to the counter, looked the server in the eye, and waved his hand over the entire baseball team.

"Fill 'em up," he roared. "Fill 'em up."

Hearing Coach Wilcox bellow, "Fill 'em up," was the biggest act of generosity I had ever witnessed. These days we drink soda as if it's water, but back then, drinking pop was something special. Three sodas on the same day was practically unheard of. And offering unlimited root beer to each member of a baseball team—well, that was flat out beyond belief. Coach Wilcox rewrote the laws of the universe right before our eyes. He would not have surprised me more if he had arbitrarily suspended the law of gravity.

I looked over at Kirby and briefly wondered what it must be like to have your dad coach your team. Every time Kirby stood knock-kneed in front of that dusty plate, his father was there to watch. He didn't miss a single swing, a single ball, or a single hit. After the game Kirby did not need to recount the run-saving catch or the stolen base; his dad was there all along, watching every move.

That was not true of my dad. His attendance at games was an uncommon occurrence. If I had a relative in the stands, it was usually Aunt Edna. She didn't know a baseball from a beachball, but she was willing to come.

I cannot pretend it didn't hurt when I saw many other boys with their dads on camping trips and in the bleachers at games. But as I grew older I realized that the most important thing my dad ever taught me is that there are more important things than me. Though he loved me passionately, and though I believe he would have died, if need be, defending me, he never pretended that the universe revolved solely around me. God had called him to share the gospel, and our togetherness would have to be on God's field of endeavor rather than my field of dreams.

In fact, instead of taking an entire baseball team out for root beers, my father was more likely to miss a turn.

MISSING THE TURN

In days past, billboards played a larger role in advertising than they do today, though in some states, billboards are still all over the place. I can remember us kids reading one vivid, blue-and-white billboard and shouting out, "Dairy Queen, five miles! Can we stop, Dad?"

"We'll see," was always his reply.

A few minutes later another billboard displayed the glories of that ice-cream cone with the curl on top. "Three miles, Dad," we all reminded him, "just three miles!"

My father smiled and nodded—and kept driving with an iron grip.

Then, in big black letters so large a grown man could fit inside the Q, a giant billboard proclaimed, "DAIRY QUEEN—turn here."

"Did you get that, Dad?" we asked.

"Get what?" my father said.

"The Dairy Queen, it's right here." We looked anxiously at the brightly lit and colorfully painted DQ stand, drawing perilously near, considering the speed with which my father was bearing ahead.

"What Dairy Queen?"

"The Dairy Queen we've been talking about for five miles."

"Oh, is that coming up?"

"Yes!" we screamed, "it's right there!" moaning as we pointed to a restaurant that was now fifty yards behind us.

"I'm sorry," Dad would say, "I guess we missed it."

Some might say that my dad missed much more than a restaurant. They might even suggest that his priorities were not in order, but I have a different take on it.

Sure, we only rarely ate out. And yes, my dad missed a lot of baseball games. But in doing both, he pointed to a mission that reordered our family's priorities, a world of the spirit devoted to ministry where the resources did not allow us the luxuries we sometimes consider necessities today.

Please understand, my father was not disinterested in his kids. Far from it. And he did not miss our baseball games just so he could go bowling or earn another quick buck. That wasn't it at all. A kid notices the difference; at least I did.

In fact, my father regularly invited me to go on ministry trips with him. All the focus today is on having dads enter their children's world, but my father invited me to enter *his*. As I debated whether to go—is this trip worth missing a game, or a camping trip, or a bicycle ride?—I knew it was really a question of whether I was going to be involved in the mission God had given my dad.

More often than not, I chose to go, and this habit of going with Dad persisted beyond my child and teen years. One trip in particular became a seminal moment in my life, a moment that shaped me into a different person. You know what I mean: you walk a little differently and you breathe a little deeper afterward because a new dimension has been opened up to you as old limits are discarded like yesterday's newspaper.

It was 1965, I was twenty-three years old, and my mother and father had been commissioned to travel around the world to minister at mission outposts where some of my father's former students were stationed. My mother was the kind of woman who was occasionally willing to endure flying, but she never relished it; and the thought of an around-the-world trip, all of it by air, was more than she could suffer. So my father invited me to go with him instead.

This trip rewrote my entire childhood. When I saw the students' faces light up once they caught their first glimpse of my father in many years; when I witnessed firsthand the global impact these students were making; when I heard the testimonies of how my father had introduced people to the Lord and trained

More Important Things Than Me

individuals who had ushered thousands of others into the kingdom of God, I no longer grieved over the empty bench at the baseball park or the vacant space next to me in a camping tent. It was clear to me that my dad had used his time wisely.

Earlier I thought that while working to construct the kingdom of God, my father was ignoring me. It turns out he was *building* me. His unwavering focus on the Son of God had radically challenged the son of his wife. It had a bigger impact on me than afternoon walks in the park, that's for sure.

NO PAIN, NO GAIN

There is an irony behind all this truth: while the most important thing my father ever taught me was that there are more important things than me, one of those "more important things" is the story of Jesus, who by sacrificing His life on my behalf said to me that *I* was one of the most important things!

My father provided me with a sense of worth by pointing me toward a God who valued me, who cherished me, and who even died for me. If I ever questioned, "Do I matter? Am I important?" all I needed to do was look at my father's mission in life, remember the redemptive purpose of Christ, and be reassured.

When a father adheres to an important mission or a noble aspiration, he has an incredible opportunity to invite his family to participate in that challenge. The sometimes difficult truth behind this is that sacrifice is an important element of any successful endeavor.

The modern athlete puts it in terms of "no pain, no gain." Looked at this way, pain itself is not bad, *provided it is being endured for a higher purpose.* If my dad had been absent for selfish ends, we would have been heartbroken and felt diminished.

But necessary pain endured for noble reasons is an entirely different matter. Understanding this allowed Janet and me to accept some of the hard sacrifice required of our own children when I entered public service. Now that the roles are reversed, I have learned that absence on the part of a parent is as painful to the parent as it is to the child, but the mutually endured sacrifice can have eternal meaning for both.

I remembered back to my own childhood, when my father could be gone as long as two months at a time, particularly in the summers when my parents traveled all over the country doing a "circuit" of camp meetings. I was in my young teens, and during those summers I was raised primarily by my grandfather.

Was I emotionally crippled because of those summers? Absolutely not. In fact, I believe I was made stronger. I learned how to handle stress successfully in a loving and supportive environment.

Jesus Himself faced family dislocation. Remember when He

cried out to His heavenly Father, "My God, My God, why have You forsaken Me?"[11] If the Trinity could be interrupted for the purposes of forgiveness, reconciliation, and redemption; if Jesus was willing to endure what felt like a spiritual dislocation from His Father; then who am I to insist that my family never endure similar sacrifice?

The glory of Jesus' death on the cross—the reason we refer to *Good* Friday instead of *Tragic* Friday—is that His death represents pain with meaning, pain with redemption. If Jesus had died without purpose, Christians would talk about "Black Friday." There would be nothing good about it.

The unique aspect of Christ's experience on the cross was that it was the sacrifice with meaning for every man, woman, and child who had ever lived or who would ever be born in the years to come. It meant so much that we literally break history by the birth of Christ, counting all the years before His coming as one epoch, and every year after as yet another.

These lessons came together when, as a twenty-three year old on that round-the-world trip, I watched my father closely, seeing how his eyes danced with the good reports given by his former students. I drank in the deep, soul-felt laughter that comes when genuine relationships are renewed after many years. I followed the footsteps of a man who clearly knew the fulfillment of a noble, eternal mission. And I wanted to be like that man.

Dad's devotion to the spiritual over the material, and the eternal over the temporal, required great sacrifice. There were moments of isolation and uncertainty. But at an early age I was liberated by the understanding that there were more important things than me. Instead of resisting that thought, I wanted to get lost in it and find a purpose more important than myself.

Twenty-two

YOUR OPINION, PLEASE

"Dear Santa," the fifth-grade girl's letter began, "I have not been a really good girl. I have been praying for a daddy for almost three years. Now I am asking you for a daddy so my mom, daddy, and I can go to the park and walk around. Please bring me a daddy for Christmas. Thank you."

We often hear how materialistic kids are these days; all they want, we say, are more toys, more things, more junk. But then you read a real letter such as this, and you realize that all some kids want is a walk in the park with both a dad and a mom. They want intimacy. They want family.

We cannot overestimate the power of an active, engaged parent and what that can mean to a child. This is true on so many levels. My father did more than invite me into his world; he invited me into his mind. It was a fascinating journey and his way of telling me, even at a young age, that I mattered.

"WHAT DO YOU THINK?"

"So, what did you think, John?"

I had just heard my father address a group of college students, and he asked my opinion. You know what this says to an adolescent boy? It says, "I value your judgment. I want to know what you think. There is worth in your discernment. I think you have a contribution to make."

This had an effect on me that my father probably did not intend. Whenever I traveled with him, I made sure I listened very closely. I knew he would quiz me about whether there was any tension or contradiction or even irony between any of the concepts he expressed. Knowing this was coming, I wanted to be able to reflect thoughtfully, so I listened as if nothing else mattered.

Many dads today have a difficult time getting their sons to listen to them, but my dad figured out that one of the best ways to get me to listen was by *listening to me first.* He asked my opinion. He got into my mind, so that I wanted to get into his. In short, he asked me for help.

He started this when I was at a very young age, even before I was ten. I saw him do it with other people too.

"John," he would say, "I've seldom learned anything from

an argument, but I've learned an awful lot from vigorous discussions." Instead of fighting with people, Dad wanted to learn from them. He understood that we all need each other. I saw a profound picture of this during one of my performances in Branson, Missouri.

ONE-HAND CLAPPING

Country music has swept across America, but nowhere has its invasion been so thorough as in Branson. Invited to sing at a gala supporting efforts to reduce and prevent birth defects, I was the token politician in a galaxy of stars like Wayne Newton and Christi Lane.

Perhaps it was the surprise of my raspy voice and my rocky composition that energized the crowd: some stood, others stomped, but everyone clapped. Everyone, that is, except a paraplegic in a wheelchair; he had only one arm he could move. His head nodded, his eyes danced, but with only one hand, clapping was beyond his reach.

A woman seated next to him saw what was going on and literally "lent that boy a hand." She reached over, and the two began clapping hands together. What a compelling scene, one person helping another, both becoming more beautiful in the process. It was tough to keep singing!

None of us are perfectly whole. Each of us needs completion.

A little girl's family needs a dad. My dad needed a son to give him feedback. This young man needed another hand to clap. All of us can supply the necessary "other hand" to round out and perfect the capacity of someone else.

That Branson couple's joint effort at clapping had all the harmony and brilliance of a symphony of angels doing the work of God. My dad's simple request, "What did you think about what I said?" had all the wisdom of the prophets. He looked at an adolescent boy and was willing to let that boy "round him out."

Do yourself a favor. The next time you're driving with someone, and you see that faraway look in their eyes, and you wonder what's going on in their heads—*ask them.*

Twenty-three

AS THE SEASONS CHANGE

Growing up I never imagined that I would one day need a man to work five days a week just to organize my schedule, let alone have an after-hours recording that goes something like this: "Hello, I'm Andy Beach, scheduler for Senator John Ashcroft. If you would like to request an appointment, please fax your request to the following number. . . ."

But as the years passed, my busy dad became a little less busy, and I became more so.

It happens to every generation. When the boy is young, he wants to spend all day with his dad, but his dad has too many things to do. Once the boy inches toward thirty or forty, the father is often heading into his sixth or seventh decade. Just as the father is winding down his career, the boy—now a man— is taking off, and the roles are reversed.

This is where the bedrock nature of philosophies is confirmed or discarded. It was easy for my dad to teach me that there were more important things in the world than me when I was a young boy, but now that he was a widower, would the tables be turned? Would he want me to pretend that there could never be more important things in the world than him?

My father passed this test with his usual aplomb. In fact, even in his latter, potentially lonelier years, Dad was passionate about taking pressure off people.

"John," he'd say, "I'd really love to see you this weekend, but please don't come if it's too difficult for you or if it complicates your life; we'll be able to get together another time."

When he invited us over, we knew we were incredibly welcome, but he would always leave us with a gracious way out. My father understood that a generous dinner invitation can unintentionally make a busy life more complicated, so he was adamant: "Come when you can and leave when you want to."

In this my father carried his level of ministry into his fellowship, creating an unselfish hospitality that sought genuinely to give, not to receive. So often it's the other way around, and people can make you suffer and feel obligated, all in the name of hospitality.

Some elderly parents do this to their children. "My kids

never come to see me anymore," they moan, and their elderly friends commiserate with them. And when their kids do visit, these same parents latch on and cling until the will to escape is exceeded only by the will to avoid coming back. The parents won't let them go without a hundred pounds of guilt added to their already complicated lives, and then they wonder why the kids are not eager to return.

A thirty-five year old is wide-eyed with the world finally beginning to open up to him. For once he is respected and paid for doing meaningful work. He has probably achieved a certain sense of responsibility. His own kids are counting on him; a company might have given him an office; a bank has been willing to lend him hundreds of thousands of dollars to buy a house.

These things look a little less shiny to us empty nesters. We're more likely to be drawn to the reconnection afforded to us by family; even a top-level strategy meeting cannot compare with taking the grandkids to McDonald's.

It never occurred to us that the day would come when relationships and family are more thrilling than landing a new account, just as it does not occur to our grown children. We can choose to make this shortsightedness a berating burden that our children must carry, or we can carry it for them by releasing them into their own domain.

I have worked hard to extend this freedom to my kids. Since my schedule is so tight, the pockets of time in which I can visit them in Missouri are much smaller than I would like. Even so, I can't expect them suddenly to drop their lives just to assuage their dad's schedule.

"Jay," I'll often say to my son when he comes to our farm, "I'm thrilled you're here, but whenever you have to go, feel free to leave." I appreciated the liberating effect this had on me, and I want my kids to enjoy it as well.

My father's soft, welcoming invitations and openhanded hospitality testified to the heartfelt nature of his teaching. Not only was he willing to show me that there are more important things in the world than me, but he was also willing to accept that at times there were more important things in the world than him.

That's not a bad philosophy for life.

Twenty-four

STAYING ALIVE

———

$\mathcal{I}$ stole a quick glance back and noticed that his legs were skinnier than they used to be. Getting a read on the speed of the boat—nearly thirty miles per hour—I checked the water in front of me. It was clear, so I looked over my shoulder once again. I saw that my father's hair definitely looked thinner, and his arms were not as well defined as they once were, but he was still in the height of his glory, water-skiing on the Lake of the Ozarks.

He was seventy-eight at the time!

My father was not a "jock," but he remained active until the day he died. When he went to Mexico for a honeymoon with his second wife, Mabel, he decided to try a new hobby.

Parasailing.

Even though my father was diagnosed with diabetes in his early sixties, he refused to declare his life at an end—or even to slow down. He squeezed meaning and faith and purpose out of every hour God gave him. It's almost poetic that he died on the road, at my brother Bob's house in Kansas City.

I have known people who reached a certain age and made either a conscious or unconscious decision to quit living and wait to die, but my father practically put death on hold. He never stopped learning, he never stopped teaching, and he kept physically active until God took him home. And he is not alone.

AN ACTIVE MIND

At ninety-four, neuropsychiatrist Leopold Hofstatter has spent seventy-five years unraveling the mysteries of the human brain. At an age when many hope to remember the names and faces of great-grandchildren, Dr. Hofstatter is still doing research at the Missouri Institute of Mental Health. An accomplished pianist, he also performs at local churches.

Dr. Hofstatter cares for his brain by regularly taxing it. He studies languages in addition to medicine. He works six days a week. He neither smokes nor drinks because he wants to protect the neurons that facilitate thought.

Because of the sharpness of his intellect, he is a critical component of an Alzheimer's research project at Washington University. Though more than 50 percent of the population over eighty-five suffer from a significant loss of cognitive function, Dr. Hofstatter has suffered no such loss. Based on his own research and experience (and who has the audacity to question him?), he believes that mental exercise has been the key to his maintaining healthy brain function throughout his life.

Even before I heard of this renowned doctor, I had developed a profound appreciation for lifelong, continuing education, because my dad taught me that the process of learning something new can be tremendously uplifting and invigorating.

That's why I'm a fan of the "discovery" school of education. When education focuses exclusively on comprehension, an important spiritual element is lost. I like to think of an educated person as someone who has become addicted to the thrill of discovery.

The "Aha!" experience keeps us alive. It's something my father treasured. Though my father regretted his absence of formal education at an earlier time in his life, he made up for it by staying fully alive through additional lifelong learning.

If someone is feeling prematurely old, the remedy is to buy a telescope, experience a new culture, or work through a college textbook. Instead of mentally and emotionally retiring, living in the past, try "retreading" and looking toward the future.

RETREAD, DON'T RETIRE

Zero windchill, icy sleet, and a steel-gray dawn set the stage for the Springfield Veterans Day parade breakfast. I sat down at the VFW table and joined the chat. One of the vets said, "John, know how old Charlie is next to you?"

I stole a quick glance at Charlie and shook my head.

"One hundred!" the first man exclaimed.

At this, Charlie protested. "Am not," he said. "Only ninety-nine. Won't be one hundred for another two months."

Having been thus introduced, Charlie, a man with a long past, began talking about the future. A Democrat for every day of the twentieth century, he was thinking about switching. Impatient with the federally mandated fifty-five-mile-per-hour speed limit, he complained about the speeding ticket he got driving back from California. And this almost-centenarian proclaimed, "The deficit's got to be controlled; it's ruining my future."

Charlie reminded me of my dad. Eighteen years after a person's normal retirement age, Dad was actively working and ministering. When his body began to give out and forced him to slow down, he focused on ministering to me.

At this point in his life, his vocation was preparing his children, and this sense of spiritual mission kept him alive perhaps longer than he would have lived otherwise. He could see the end. He told us he was going to make my January 1995 swearing-in to the U.S. Senate. Interestingly enough, he never committed to my daughter's wedding, which was coming up in April.

Somehow he knew.

Our spirits need purpose to keep functioning, in the same way our bodies need food to keep moving. That's why retirement just wasn't in Dad's vocabulary. For him to step prematurely into retirement would have been tantamount to stepping into a premature death. When mission defines who you are, there is no you when the mission dies.

My father and Charlie both made a conscious decision that they would not retire—they would retread and keep on living. They kept their spirits alive with a strong mission. It's a lesson we would all do well to learn. We can begin practicing this by living with open eyes.

OPEN YOUR EYES

Perception is a vital sign of life. While we're seeing, we're learning; and while we're learning, we're living.

There is a twisting farm road near our place in Greene County. At the right time of year, in the right weather, tarantulas make a crossing there. Most drivers miss seeing these hairy creatures, but I like to stop and watch. I have been known to pick up one or two and take them home to Janet. She screams enough to make me feel it's a worthwhile endeavor, but she does not appreciate it. It's a family joke that I enjoy and she endures.

Dad encouraged me to live with open eyes, to stay fully

alive through 100 percent vision. Every day most of us pass sights of wonder and beauty, but we have put blinders on our souls and miss the spiritual nurture these treasures bring.

On a road trip with a friend, I was driving by a field when I saw more than a dozen wild turkeys off in the distance. It's practically automatic: my foot hit the brake and I pointed them out. My friend had never seen turkeys in the wild before, so I pulled over, and he chased after them to get a better look. He did not get very close, of course—turkeys are easily spooked. But here's the thing: he saw them.

"How will he ever use that?" you might ask. That's the wrong question. He saw something new. He enlarged his life. He stayed fully alive.

Another element to staying alive is staying active.

STAYING ACTIVE

During my time as governor, I had the pleasure of naming Audrey Stubbard of Independence as "Missouri's Older Worker of the Year." Audrey was a victim of a mandatory retirement rule in 1961; but, like my father and Charlie, she decided to retread instead of retire.

As a person well past retirement age, Audrey tackles one of a newspaper's toughest jobs: proofreader. Starting before 7:30 each day, she tears into the text, studiously looking for errors and misspellings that litter the copy. As I write this, Audrey is still going strong at the age of 101!

The paper holds a birthday luncheon for Audrey each year, and she usually says about the same thing: "Thank you for keeping me alive. If I couldn't come to work, I'm sure I would have died."

Audrey has spent *four decades* after retirement catching the newspaper's errors, but in doing that, she may have pointed out our society's biggest error of all—dying before our time.

It's a matter of stewardship, really. If you hand someone a crystal vase for a present and they start tossing it in the air, you get the feeling that they may be going to waste what you've given them. We do the same thing to God, foolishly cutting our lives short by adopting destructive habits and by going to sleep, spiritually, long before our appointed time to die.

Dad was not like that. Like Audrey, like Charlie, and like Dr. Hofstatter, he stayed fully engaged in the game of life. He did not let up until the lights were turned off and his Coach showed up to take him home.

CHAPTER

Twenty-five

A GIVER

*F*or people like my father, giving is not a hobby, a virtue, or a religious practice. It's a way of life.

Dad gave things away with a passion. He never let people leave without placing something in their hands. He even developed a signature gift, designing a plaque that he produced for the sole purpose of giving away. The calligraphy on the plaque reads: "'As long as he sought the LORD, God made him to prosper' (2 Chronicles 26:5)."

Since the plaques are custom designed, you can't miss them. If you see one, you know it came from my father. I have seen these plaques all over the world. I even saw one in Hong Kong!

There is something simply profound about putting in so much time, effort, and expense to make a signature gift. In this, Dad has left a fascinating legacy for his children and grandchildren.

You do not get this serious about giving if you view it as

simply another obligation. The secret uncovered by my father was that giving can be tremendous fun—you never know when a gift is going to come back to bless you. On a few occasions, I have experienced this joy of "returned" giving.

GIFTS THAT COME BACK

I was invited to speak to a group called Technet, a network of technology-oriented companies that have collaborated to educate government officials on the intricacies of emerging technology. That's a fancy way of saying they have banded together to make sure Congress doesn't confound their industry with crazy laws!

Before that morning I might have had trouble recognizing the young man who introduced me. If someone had asked me, "Do you know this man?" I might not have been sure. We were in Palo Alto, California, half a country away from my home state.

Yet when he introduced me, he used a personal anecdote. "When Senator Ashcroft was a young man and I was a kid," this man recounted, "he taught me how to water-ski."

I was stunned. It was like seeing my dad's plaque in Hong Kong. How did that gift get all the way over here?

That was at eight in the morning. By eight o'clock that night I had traveled to Bakersfield and then on to Costa Mesa, where I had another meeting. Once again I was introduced, and once again the emcee recounted something that took me completely by surprise. "We've loved this John Ashcroft for a long time," he said. "As a matter of fact, a number of years ago, he taught my wife to water-ski."

Twice in one day! Things come back to you. It's amazing. I did not recall teaching either of these individuals how to water-ski, but there it was, embedded as a meaningful memory in their lives. I do remember our motto—"Have boat, will pull"—led us to yank a lot of people in the sport of waterskiing.

I frequently hear similar stories about gifts given by my father. Virtually everywhere I go, people come up and speak to me of something he did. This has become so commonplace, it's hard to be surprised anymore.

One weekend I visited Vermont with Senator Jim Jeffords. "If you want to go to church tomorrow," Senator Jeffords offered, "I'll go wherever you want to attend."

"Well, let's go to the local Assembly of God," I suggested.

Senator Jeffords and I had barely sat down in the pew when people started coming up to me, saying how happy they were to see me because they had known my father. When the special guest minister introduced his wife, she came to the pulpit and said, "I'm pleased to be here, and I'm especially delighted to see Senator Ashcroft here. In the early '40s, my father was seriously ill. The doctors could not foresee a recovery, and everything looked pretty grim until a young minister came in and prayed for Dad, and he was healed. That young minister's name was J. Robert Ashcroft, Senator Ashcroft's father."

Time stopped as I sat in the pew, the '90s folding back half a century as I imagined my father, at the time younger than I am now, diligently serving and trusting in God as a young minister. Fifty years later, his body was buried under the earth, his soul in heaven, but the testimonies he had left behind were still inspiring folks around the world.

The Bible reminds us that the sins of the fathers will be visited on their children, but that Sunday I realized how the *virtues* of a father can enrich his children. A father's gifts keep giving a spiritual inheritance.

THE MEANING OF GIVING

Though I cannot paint myself as being a great giver, I have noticed an interesting dynamic: I have never been sorry for anything I have ever given away (the same is not true concerning everything I have kept or purchased). And some of my most meaningful moments have resulted from giving.

I remember when a relatively young woman, who worked for me while I was governor, was dying of cancer. I went into her hospital room and was greatly moved by the inevitability of her impending death. She had been such a hard worker and she had served the citizens of Missouri so well, I wanted to do something for her in the last precious days of her life.

"Is there anything I can do for you?" I asked.

She smiled. "I'd really love some chocolate chip cookies."

That afternoon I returned to the governor's mansion and started assembling the necessary ingredients.

"What are you doing?" the staff cook wanted to know.

"I'm making chocolate chip cookies."

"I can do that for you."

I cleared the kitchen right then and there. This was something I wanted to do myself. It just wouldn't be the same if somebody else did the baking.

But then—it always happens this way—the act of giving started paying me back. The process of baking those cookies—a small thing—allowed me to process my prayers for her family and work through my anger at the cigarettes that had needlessly shortened her life. That time in the kitchen became a holy time, a culinary prayer.

I used my favorite recipe and slightly underbaked the cookies so they would be good and moist. I like to make them small, so they'll stack in a Pringles' can, and I delivered the cookies later that day.

How many afternoons have I lived that have now been forgotten? Too many to count, that's for sure, but I will never forget that afternoon in the kitchen, baking cookies for a woman who was dying. It was such a little thing, but as I said earlier, the little things give life meaning far beyond their size.

WHO IS GENEROUS?

The key to giving is in the giver. We need to be careful, because generosity has been greatly misconstrued in our day. Political liberals often take the admonition to be generous in giving as an admonition directed toward the government. In actuality, it's the reverse.

Real givers are people who enjoy giving away their *own* money. Beware the "generosity" of those who make a living giving away *other people's* money.

A good example of a positive giver is Charles Feeney, a businessman from New Jersey who made a fortune in duty-free airport shops. Though his net earnings have been estimated in the billions, Feeney is actually worth only a fraction of that. Why?

He gives most of his money away.

Billionaire Charles Feeney does not own a house. Or a car. He even sits in the cheap, cramped seats on airplanes. After rearing five children, he decided that he had enough money, so he started systematically getting rid of it. He began funding humanitarian projects in Third World countries. He provided research grants to hospitals and universities; one worthwhile charity received a cool thirty million dollars in a single gift.

Feeney was not doing this for publicity. He went to a great deal of trouble to conceal his generosity, even going so far as using cashier's checks to protect his anonymity. It was not until he sold his business interest that his record of ultragenerous giving became a matter of public record.

Another great giver is Lyle Worley of Springfield, Missouri. Though wealthy in spirit, Lyle isn't even close to being a billionaire. Or millionaire. But he, too, has learned the secret of giving. The Red Cross honored him in 1996 for giving more than five thousand hours of volunteer effort, and at the time, he was only forty-eight years old. A versatile community-service dynamo, Worley has helped the Red Cross with emergency response, disaster relief, and their famous blood drives. He also pitched in to help his chapter install a new computer system.

In his "spare" time Mr. Worley directs a program for hearing-impaired children and helps out with the Boy Scouts.

Charles Feeney and Lyle Worley demonstrate a standard of giving that goes so far beyond the average that they become virtually otherworldly in their orientation. What's their secret?

It's the same secret learned by my father. Lyle Worley says he simply discovered years ago that helping others is more rewarding than spending time on himself. He has taken our Lord's words—"It is more blessed to give than to receive"[12]— at face value and found them to be true.

A syndicated columnist wrote that Americans "have more money, but less virtue. We have more of things disposable and less of things eternal." Maybe, as we learn to give, we will find something far more valuable than the money we so vainly strive after and so tenaciously cling to. We might find that the spirit of giving not only helps sustain us, but it can outlive us.

Just ask Charles Feeney, Lyle Worley—and my dad.

CHAPTER

Twenty-six

MAJORS AND MINORS

$\mathcal{D}$o you think illegal drugs are "moderately" dangerous to society?

Do you believe it is "somewhat" important to have a personal relationship with God?

Do you believe it is "sort of" a risk to sell nuclear technology to Communist-ruled China?

And let me ask you this: if you're serving in combat, would you want your fellow soldiers to be "moderately" brave?

Me neither.

The labels "moderate" and "conservative" are sometimes abused in today's society. By some jaundiced standards, moderation is good under virtually any circumstance. And *extreme* means "undesirable," no matter what values are at stake.

In reality, there are some things we must be strongly, even passionately, committed to. (I don't apologize for being unyielding when I speak on behalf of a balanced budget or in opposition to big government or in favor of protecting the lives of unborn children.)

My father said, "Don't major in the minors or minor in the majors." This may be some of the best folksy advice I have ever received. We can waste so much energy putting undue emphasis on trivial things that when something arises that really does matter, it gets drowned in the deluge of our causes.

In politics this is a daily challenge. All the good groups in the world (and a few bad ones) bring their causes, purposes, or bills to my office virtually every day, and if I don't happen to speak out on their particular concern at least once a week, my integrity may be questioned: "What's happened to you? Why are you silent? Don't you care?"

What some of these groups do not understand is the necessity of what we call "staying on message." When elected officials run their offices like bumblebees, buzzing from flower to flower, they risk getting nothing done. In terms of physics, it goes like this: if you don't concentrate your force, you might not penetrate the wall. I can't possibly speak out on everything. Some issues have other senators as their champions, in which case I may stand behind them as a strong supporter. On other issues, I'm out front and center; but no single senator can be the standard-bearer on every issue that's important.

What all of us must do is determine the primary emphasis of our calling, and then stay on course, emphasizing it over and over again. A good friend of mine understands this. He tells me he has 365 titles but only two speeches; regardless of what group or issue he's asked to address, he is going to stay on message.

This is as essential for parenting as it is for politics. Dad repeated the same things throughout his entire life: the importance of the spiritual over the material; the priority of the eternal over the temporal; the need to marshal all of your resources to participate in God's redemptive work. Because he stayed so focused, it was impossible to be around him for any length of time and not know what he believed in.

We have to ask ourselves: what do our kids perceive as the primary message of our lives? What gets us really passionate? A mistake on our grocery bill? A new television set? A "must-see" TV show? What do others see us majoring in?

If we're smart, we'll major in majors. We'll take a time-out and *choose* what is really important rather than just falling into it.

CHAPTER
Twenty-seven

STRUGGLING TO KNEEL

---

*T*hough we all enjoy the brilliant array of colors in the fall, few of us understand the process that changes a tree's color. As the hours of sunlight grow shorter, the tree produces less green chlorophyll. As the green of this natural chemical departs from the trees, the leaves are finally able to reveal their natural color. It's not until the chlorophyll runs out in the fall that the true glory of nature's spectacular colors is visible.

Much like a mighty tree, my dad's true colors were the most vivid at the end of his life. When he had just hours left to live, I truly saw my father at his brightest, clearest, and finest. It was a day I will never forget.

THE SPIRIT OF WASHINGTON

Before each of my inaugurations as governor, I asked that

there be a special time where friends and officials would join together to invite the presence of God both in the inaugural festivities and in the administration I would direct. In a personal and public way, I wanted to signal my individual dependence on God and our corporate dependence on the mercy of the Almighty. In 1985 and 1989, Missourians from all walks of life and every corner of the state attended these services of consecration and dedication.

The night before I was sworn in to the Senate in 1995, my father arranged for some close friends and family—maybe fifteen to twenty people—to gather for dinner. My father eyed a piano in the corner of the room and said, "John, why don't you play the piano and we'll sing?"

"Okay, Dad. You name it, I'll play it."

"Let's sing, 'We Are Standing on Holy Ground.'"

It was one of my father's favorites, but he was not engaging in some sentimental ploy by suggesting it. As I would later learn, a profound purpose undergirded his request.

After the song, I eased away from the piano keys and found myself thinking out loud. "We're standing here having a good time," I said, "but I really wish we were in a dedication service."

The impending responsibilities of the Senate were already weighing heavily on me. I did not have an inflated view of my importance as a senator, but I was not lackadaisical about it either.

The people of Missouri had sent me to the Senate to represent them, and I wanted to do so with integrity and character.

My lifelong friend, Dick Foth, spoke up. "We can do something about a dedication service, John."

At Dick's suggestion, we gathered early the next morning at a house not far from the Capitol. It was a beautiful house, decorated in Early American style, and maintained by a group of friends for the express purpose of bringing members of Congress together for spiritual enrichment.

We began by chatting informally and then sang a hymn or two. At the time I did not realize how weak my father was, but he had been losing weight through the months of November and December and had told an acquaintance of his, "I'm hanging on by a thread, and it's a thin thread at that, but I'm going to see John sworn into the Senate."

As we talked, the earnestness of my father's voice suddenly commanded everyone's attention. "John," Dad said, "please listen carefully." My children and I fixed our focus on Dad. My brother Bob moved to the edge of his seat. Dick Foth and the others leaned in.

"The spirit of Washington is arrogance," my dad said, "and the spirit of Christ is humility. Put on the spirit of Christ. Nothing of lasting value has ever been accomplished in arrogance."

The room was absolutely quiet. All of us were absorbed by what my father had said, and we awaited what he was struggling to say next.

"Someday I hope that someone will come up to you as you're fulfilling your duties as a senator, tug on your sleeve, and say, 'Senator, your spirit is showing.'"

There could be no more lighthearted banter after that. We were living a truly profound moment.

Back when I was eight years old, my father had used a breathtaking dive in an old Piper Cub to convince me that my actions had great consequence; now, nearly half a century later, he wanted me to remember that *how* I did what I did would have eternal impact.

After we discussed my father's words, I finally asked that we have a time of solemn prayer.

The ancient kings of Israel, David and Saul, were anointed as they undertook their administrative duties, as were some leaders in the early church. My denomination frequently follows this practice. Accordingly, I was anointed prior to each of my terms as governor.

"It's too bad we don't have any oil," I said.

"Let's see if there's something in the kitchen," my father suggested.

Dick Foth disappeared to the kitchen where Janet Potter

gave him a tiny bowl of Crisco oil. We chuckled about that, but my father assured us, "The oil itself isn't important, except as a symbol of the spirit of God."

I knelt in front of the sofa where my father was seated, and everyone gathered around me. Most placed a hand on my head, shoulders, or back. Everyone was standing when I noticed my father lunging, swinging his arms, trying to lift himself out of the couch, one of those all-enveloping pieces of furniture that tends to bury you once you sit in it. Given my father's weakness—a damaged heart operating at less than one-third capacity—getting out of that couch was taking a major-league effort.

Dad was not making much progress. I felt terrible. Knowing he did not have strength to spare, I said, "Dad, you don't have to struggle to stand and pray over me with these friends."

"John," my father answered, *"I'm not struggling to stand, I'm struggling to kneel."*

I was overwhelmed. Some statements are so profound they take awhile to sink in; others hit you with the force of a nuclear explosion, and I thought my father's words might vaporize me on the spot. I had a thousand reflections about that statement in the first half second, as if my father's insight had suddenly upgraded my mind from a 286 to a Pentium processor.

Buried in my thoughts was a good measure of shame,

but it was a good shame, the kind of shame that arises when you realize you have vastly underestimated the character of someone or his actions. It is so much more noble to kneel than to stand.

It was wonderful that everybody else in the room had taken valuable time out of their day to be with me and to stand and pray for me. But I became keenly aware that my father was operating not out of mere generosity or benevolence. He was conveying a message of eternal value and impact.

He was not struggling to stand, he was struggling to kneel.

I was taken back to those early mornings half a century before when I slipped underneath my father and joined him on his knees. He prayed then that we would do noble things. Now, still on his knees, he was taking me there.

I was overwhelmed, humbled, and inspired all at once. As the next unpredictable hours unfolded, his wise words would gain even more profound meaning.

LAST WORDS

After my swearing-in, Dad's inspiring words accompanied me like a pleasant and polite companion, supporting me from the background while other concerns demanded my immediate attention.

That night Janet and I settled into our little one-and-a-half-room apartment over a one-car garage in an alley just off Second

Street in Washington, D.C. We had chosen it because it was near the Hart Building, site of my Senate office, though it lacked a few essentials, like a phone.

The change from Missouri could not have been more pronounced. Not only did I miss the Show-Me State, but it takes a while to get used to windows and doors covered by iron bars. The weight of the swearing-in and the festivities surrounding the assumption of a new office had taken their toll, however, so it didn't take much for me to get lulled into a deep sleep.

A raucous rattling of our door's iron bars awakened me in the dead of night. I was familiar with the sound of roosters crowing, cows baying, dogs barking, and perhaps an old truck rattling by, but I had never been startled out of sleep by such a sound.

Was somebody trying to break in? Or was this just some kid trying to make a nuisance of himself?

Janet jumped out of bed, wedged her fingers between the blinds, and looked into the alley. "It's Dick Foth," she exclaimed.

"No," I said, "it's my dad."

Both Janet and I realized my dad was not in the alley. But I knew there was only one reason Dick would rattle my door in the still of night.

It has been said that a man is not a man until his father is gone. If this was what manhood felt like, I had real questions about whether I was up to it.

This was a sobering start to my Senate career, I'll tell you that much. As Dick and I talked, he said, "John, there's something you ought to know. This was not a surprise to your dad."

"What do you mean?"

"Yesterday, your father pulled me aside and said, 'Dick, I want you to assure me that when John gets to his assigned offices, you will have prayer with him, inviting the presence of God in those rooms.'

"I looked at your father and said, 'We'll do just that. And, as a matter of fact, we'll call you up in Springfield, put you on the speaker phone, and you can join us for the consecration.'

"John, the next thing I knew, your father grabbed me by the arm and said, 'You don't understand, I'll be with you, but I won't be in Springfield.'

"He knew what was coming, John. He knew."

The only appropriate response to a revelation like that is a silent one.

I would have cherished my father's admonition if he had lived another two decades, but there is something about a person's final words that make them particularly significant. The fact that they were some of the last words Dad ever said—"I'm not struggling to stand, I'm struggling to kneel"—seared them on my soul.

My father had only so much energy left, and he chose to spend it passing on to me his deepest understanding of life. My brother Bob said it was as if Dad knew his strength was fading fast, but he had tied a knot at the end of his life rope, determined to hang on until I entered the Senate. Once I did, he loosened his grip just a little bit. His heart made one final and valiant effort, then he was gone.

Dad knew he had prayed all his prayers, and it was time to leave the next generation in the hands of God. My father expended his last bit of precious life force and energy to assemble a gift he gave as we knelt knee to knee.

Some fathers deal with their sons eyeball-to-eyeball; others, nose-to-nose. In the end, my father dealt with me knee-to-knee.

CHAPTER

Twenty-eight

HOLY GROUND

---

*J*ust a few months after my father's death, I was at the airport, trying to board a delayed TWA flight. The agent looked at my ticket, which had a connecting flight in St. Louis, and insisted on changing it.

"You won't make your connection," he insisted. "I'm going to put you on the later flight out of St. Louis."

"What time does that flight arrive in Washington?" I asked.

"Around midnight."

I hate arriving in Washington at midnight; besides, I thought there was a good chance I could still make that tight connection in St. Louis. I looked at my watch, then glanced at my ticket one more time. "If we leave when you say we're going to leave, I'll make the connection," I argued, "and I want you to honor my ticket for the earlier connection."

"No, you *won't* make the connection," he stated flatly. "I

can't put you through if we know you'll miss the next flight. I have to schedule you for a later flight."

My temper started to rise until I heard somebody from the back of the luggage-laden line call out, "Yeah, he thinks he can do anything, because he's a senator."

That comment stopped me cold. I remembered my father's words: "Someday I hope someone will come up to you and say, 'Senator, your spirit is showing.'"

My spirit was showing all right, but it was the wrong spirit.

I backed down, and there was a latent sense of alienation in my stomach as I boarded the plane with a ticket for the later connection. I thought of all my father had taught me. Now that he was dead, I felt a new urgency to personify the principles he had held so dear. Yet in times like these, I was a poor representative at best.

I remembered my father's earnest plea that Dick Foth see to it that we invite God's presence into my new Senate office. Of course, Dad knew that God inhabits people, not mortar or stone. But by inviting God's presence into my Senate offices, my father wanted me to invite God's presence into everything I did as a senator—including boarding an airplane.

As it turned out, the connecting flight in St. Louis was also delayed, so I may have made the connection. But I had learned my lesson. There are only two times when the poison of arrogance pollutes—when you're wrong, and when you're right. It doesn't wear any better in either season.

I later handwrote a letter to the ticket agent and apologized. I knew I needed to ask forgiveness for my arrogant spirit.

And for that moment, my personal responsibility was recapturing one of the truths that held my father's intense concentration during the waning moments of his life: understanding the concept of holy ground.

"EVEN WASHINGTON . . ."

It was not an accident that my father sent me to the piano to play "We Are Standing on Holy Ground" the night before I was sworn in as a senator. We were gathered in the middle of our nation's capital, hardly a place known for its purity or piety, and my father wanted to make a statement. Just as Moses could stand in the dirt-dusted wilderness before a burning bush in Egypt—a nation which at that time was steeped in the worship of Pharaoh and other gods—and listen as God proclaimed it to be holy ground, God's own territory, so my father wanted to stand in the citadel of human power and say, "This place should be set apart for the work of the Lord."

"John," my father had told me after the piano keys had stilled, "I want you to know that even Washington can be holy ground. It's a place to hear the voice of God, and wherever you hear His voice, that ground is sanctified, or set apart. It's a place where God can call you to the highest and best."

In my father's view—and I think he was right in this—the factory floor in Detroit can be holy ground; the stock market exchange on Wall Street can be holy ground; the local elementary school; the fire hall; the Elks lodge; even the chew-'em-up-and-spit-'em-out halls of Washington, D.C.

Today, political life is often seen as unseemly, something beneath people of noble character. But it was not always this way. When Abraham Lincoln left Springfield, Illinois, to become the sixteenth president of the United States, he stood at the steps of a train car that was about to whisk him off. To a few of his friends who had assembled to watch him leave, Lincoln said, "I now leave, not knowing when, or whether ever, I may return—[This proved to be eerily prophetic. The next time Lincoln's body reached Springfield, it was encased by a casket]—with a task before me greater than that which rested upon [George] Washington. Without the assistance of that Divine Being who ever attended him, I cannot succeed. With that assistance I cannot fail. Trusting in Him, who can go with me, and remain with you and be everywhere for good, let us confidently hope that all will yet be well. To His care commending you, as I hope in your prayers you will commend me, I bid you an affectionate farewell."[13]

It never occurred to Lincoln to approach the ominous task of facing civil war without inviting God's presence and guidance. He knew the Source of his strength, so he was bent on consecrating Washington, D.C., as holy ground. That did not mean trying to turn the White House into a church or the Oval Office into a proselytizing, theological pulpit; but it did mean recognizing his and humankind's need for divine intervention.

It is against my religion to impose religion on people—and I suspect Lincoln would agree with me. But I also believe that I need to invite God's presence into whatever I'm doing, including the world of politics. Had I remained a teacher, I'm sure my dad would have wanted me to ask God's blessing over my classroom. Had I worked for the state patrol, he might have met me in my patrol car, beseeching God's presence.

Dad had an uncanny sense that imperfect, sinful human beings can be transformed inside out by the glorious and powerful presence of God. I'm nagged by the understanding that I will never be a perfect representative this side of heaven—that's why I had to write an apology to the ticket agent. But the more I invite God's presence into whatever I do, the more likely I will reflect His Spirit, and nothing is more meaningful than that.

Twenty-nine

SAYING GOOD-BYE

———

$\mathcal{J}$'m told that in the emergency room, as the physicians worked frantically to help my father remain in this world, Dad finally gave in. "Boys," he said, "you better just quit; you're hurting me more than you're helping me."

Because my father knew that he had been faithful to the strength and mission God had given him, he was willing to let go when the time came.

Accepting death is so symbolic of how he lived his life. My father perfected the art of saying good-bye. I can still vividly picture him standing in his yard, vigorously waving both hands like an airline attendant guiding a plane in—only Dad did it more aggressively, like a person stranded on an island. (Sometimes he would even wave a towel!)

We would be fifty, even a hundred yards down the road,

and he would still be waving good-bye. Only when the car inched out of sight would he finally drop his hands and go back inside.

In a sense, the way my father said good-bye was a profound way of saying hello. You knew how welcome you would be the next time you came around, because it was clear he was in no hurry to see you go. That extra forty-five seconds communicated as much as an hour on the telephone. It was a physical picture of sincere concern and true affection: "I'm here for you and completely engaged in being with you until you're absolutely out of sight."

Every time we say good-bye, we are in essence preparing to say hello for the next visit. If we leave someone in a fit of anger or tension, the next time we see them the relationship will be colored by that same anger or tension. Yet if we part with a sincere affection, the next greeting is likely to be even warmer.

This truth applies to social situations as much as it does to family relationships. When we say good-bye to an employer, a city, a club, or a church, we can choose to burn our bridges, or we can decide to leave in such a way that we would be enthusiastically welcomed back. Whenever we leave any situation, we're inevitably setting up the reunion.

Dad's active good-byes illustrated how he lived his final

hours. He continued to be my loving, teaching father until the last day of his life. Even though his strength was failing, he was not willing to let go until he faced death in the emergency room. He had promised to be there when I was sworn in to the Senate, and nothing could keep him away. As he sensed his spirit passing into eternity, he kept waving his hands, letting me know he was 100 percent with me until, finally, he slipped out of sight.

Looking back, I realize that my father left this earth the way his Lord did—giving himself to others. Even when Jesus was carrying His cross up the bloody hill of Golgotha, He paused to tell some women, "Daughters of Jerusalem, do not weep for Me, but weep for yourselves and for your children."[14]

It's amazing to me that after being tortured, mocked, ridiculed, and humiliated, Jesus could say, "Don't be sorry for Me. Think about how this might affect you."

And then, hanging on the cross, His wrists and feet pierced, His physical strength bleeding away, His battered and bruised body shutting down, Jesus rallied Himself to invite a repentant thief into paradise and to direct His friend John to care for Mary, Jesus' mother.

If people wonder how Jesus died so quickly, they fail to grasp the depths to which He poured Himself out for others. As we say good-bye to my father, I'm humbled, delighted, inspired, and challenged to see how closely his life modeled the God whom he loved.

Good-bye, Dad.

Thanks for the lessons.

And thanks for struggling to kneel.

I'm still struggling to learn.

THE LESSONS FROM A FATHER TO HIS SON

One

LIFE IS A SERIES OF CHOICES BETWEEN NOBLE ASPIRATIONS AND SELFISH INDULGENCE.

Two

ORDINARY PEOPLE CAN ACCOMPLISH EXTRAORDINARY THINGS.

Three

FOR EVERY CRUCIFIXION, THERE IS A RESURRECTION.

Four

SILENCE SOMETIMES SHOUTS.

Five

CREATIVE SELF-DOUBT FERTILIZES THE FIELD OF OPPORTUNITY.

Six

IT'S THE CONDITION OF THE HEART, NOT THE COLOR OF THE SKIN, THAT COUNTS.

Seven

NEVER EAT YOUR SEED CORN.

Eight

WHEN YOU'VE CONSIDERED ALL THE OPTIONS, WORK TO EXPAND YOUR OPTIONS.

Nine

SUCCESS FOLLOWS HARD WORK TO MAKE THE RIGHT DECISION, THEN EVEN HARDER WORK TO MAKE YOUR DECISION RIGHT.

Ten

THE VERDICT OF HISTORY WILL FOOL YOU; LET THE VERDICT OF ETERNITY FUEL YOU.

Eleven

THE LIVES OF FATHERS AND SONS ARE INTERTWINED; WHEN ONE DIES, THE OTHER IS DIMINISHED.

Twelve

IT'S IMPORTANT FOR A FATHER NOT ONLY TO PASS ON HIS STRENGTHS, WISDOM, AND INSIGHT, BUT ALSO TO MODEL HOW A SON SHOULD HANDLE WEAKNESSES, FAILURES, AND INSECURITIES.

Thirteen

WHEN YOU HAVE SOMETHING IMPORTANT TO SAY, WRITE IT DOWN.

Fourteen

WHEN MAKING DECISIONS, GOD EXPECTS US TO USE MATURE REASON AND SOUND JUDGMENT, GUIDED BY JUDEO-CHRISTIAN VALUES.

Fifteen

LITTLE THINGS MEAN A LOT.

Sixteen

THE MOST IMPORTANT THING MY DAD EVER TAUGHT ME IS THAT THERE ARE MORE IMPORTANT THINGS THAN ME.

Seventeen

I'VE NEVER BEEN SORRY FOR WHAT I'VE GIVEN AWAY, ONLY WHAT I'VE KEPT.

Eighteen

NOT ONLY DOES WHAT I DO HAVE GREAT
CONSEQUENCE, BUT *HOW* I DO WHAT I DO HAS
ETERNAL CONSEQUENCE.

Nineteen

THE MOST IMPORTANT RESPONSIBILITY OF A CULTURE IS
THE TRANSMISSION OF VALUES FROM ONE GENERATION
TO THE NEXT.

Twenty

THE PRESENCE OF GOD TRANSFORMS GRIT AND GRIME
INTO HOLY GROUND.

Twenty-one

SAYING GOOD–BYE IS A PROFOUND WAY OF BEGINNING
TO SAY HELLO.

NOTES

1. Matthew 6:14–15.
2. James Weldon Johnson, "The Creation," *God's Trombones* (New York: The Viking Press, 1927).
3. Matthew 5:11–12.
4. Luke 6:38.
5. Proverbs 29:18 KJV.
6. Matthew 19:17.
7. John 14:11.
8. Deuteronomy 30:19.
9. Rudolph Giuliani, "How New York Is Becoming the Safest Big City in America," *USA Today* magazine, Jan. 1997, 29.
10. Ibid.
11. Matthew 27:46.
12. Acts 20:35 KJV.
13. Abraham Lincoln, "Farewell Address at Springfield, Illinois, February 11, 1861," *Lincoln: Speeches, Letters, Miscellaneous Writings, Presidential Messages and Proclamations* (Library of America, vol. 2, 1989).
14. Luke 23:28.

ABOUT THE AUTHOR

*J*ohn Ashcroft of Missouri was elected to the United States Senate in 1994, winning 60 percent of the vote and carrying every county in the state. Prior to his election to the Senate, he served Missourians as their governor for two terms, winning reelection in 1988 by 64 percent, the largest percentage of any Missouri governor since the Civil War.

Ashcroft is the author of the landmark Charitable Choice provision of the new welfare reform law. This innovation allows states to work directly with charities and faith-based organizations to move people from dependence to work. He has authored other significant changes to federal law, including discipline and record-keeping reforms that strengthen the ability of schools to deal with dangerous or disruptive students; a ban on the use of federal funds for assisted suicide; and lawsuit protection for people who volunteer in their communities.

He is also the sponsor of major legislation to enact broad-based middle class tax relief by making payroll taxes deductible, thus ending an unfair double tax on work. A strong proponent of term limits, Ashcroft's determined efforts secured the first Senate vote on term limits in fifty years.

Ashcroft also is widely recognized for his innovative use of technology and the Internet. He conducted the first-ever congressional on-line petition for an issue before Congress (term limits) and has taught students in Missouri and across the country about using the Internet and on-line information as a tool of citizenship.

Ashcroft was born on May 9, 1942. He attended public schools in Springfield, Missouri, and graduated with honors from Yale University in 1964. He met his wife, Janet, at the University of Chicago Law School where they each received law degrees in 1967, and later coauthored two college textbooks. They have three children, Martha Patterson, Jay, and Andrew.

In addition to his public service, Ashcroft enjoys singing and songwriting. He is the baritone voice of The Singing Senators quartet with Senators Trent Lott, Larry Craig, and James Jeffords.